A Bird's-Eye View of Assessment

Selections from Editor's Notes

Edited by Trudy W. Banta

Assessment
UPdate
COLLECTIONS

Published by Jossey-Bass
A Wiley Imprint
989 Market Street, San Francisco, CA 94103-1741   www.josseybass.com

Jossey-Bass books and products are available through most bookstores. To contact Jossey-Bass
directly call our Customer Care Department within the U.S. at 800-956-7739, outside the
U.S. at 317-572-3986, or fax 317-572-4002.

Jossey-Bass also publishes its books in a variety of electronic formats. Some content that
appears in print may not be available in electronic books.

Library of Congress Cataloging-in-Publication Data available upon request

FIRST EDITION
PB Printing   10 9 8 7 6 5 4 3 2 1

Contents

One Bird's-Eye View of the U.S. Landscape for Assessment

Tripping Lightly Around the Globe

Selections from Trudy Banta's "Editor's Notes"

1989–2010

What a privilege it is to have the opportunity to look back over more than 20 years of contributions to *Assessment Update* and share some of my favorite columns with you! As I contemplated this pleasant task, I thought it might be difficult to identify a few distinct categories for the more than 80 of my "Editor's Notes" columns. But once I dove into the pile of issues, I discovered that wasn't hard at all. Soon I was able to sort each issue into one of four stacks. Then I went through each stack and selected the half-dozen or so columns that seemed to tell the most important stories. Winnowing that collection to a set manageable within these covers was the most challenging part of the assignment.

The Four Stacks

A persistent theme in my work in outcomes assessment has been a search for characteristics, or principles, of good practice. I've put columns related to this theme in the section "Some Things Never Change."

After finishing a book or another significant writing project, I have usually developed an essay for *AU* summarizing the contents or an aspect of my thinking that emerged from, but was not necessarily covered in, the published work. It thus seemed appropriate to call the second section "You Won't Find This in Books."

Throughout my career in assessment I have been drawn into several national initiatives focused on accountability, and of course I've described them in columns. Since mine is just one perspective on these initiatives, I've called the third section "One Bird's-Eye View of the U.S. Landscape for Assessment."

Finally, I have attempted to sample global dimensions of quality assurance/assessment by attending at least a couple of conferences in other countries each year since 1990, then writing about my observations. But I have not delved deeply into the issues in any particular country. Thus the fourth section is entitled "Tripping Lightly Around the Globe."

Some Things Never Change

The first issue of *Assessment Update* appeared in Spring 1989, and in my column in that issue I painted a picture of the current landscape of outcomes assessment in a series of broad strokes. In the second issue my essay described assessment at the three institutions considered pioneers in this arena, each of which had been profiled in Peter Ewell's *Self-Regarding Institution* (1984): Alverno College, Northeast Missouri (now Truman) State University, and the University of Tennessee, Knoxville. In these earliest contributions and in three others spanning the decade of the 1990s, it seems to me that I described many of the characteristics of effective assessment practice that we espouse today. For better or for worse, some things haven't changed. The principles we discovered and enunciated 20 years ago are as relevant as ever.

The principles described in the selected columns include:

- Engage faculty colleagues by linking assessment to activities they value, such as improving student learning, and demonstrating that they are already doing assessment as a component of their teaching.

- If you want to know how students are experiencing instruction and support services, ask them!

- A matrix can be a valuable tool to organize thinking about an assessment process, or even the entire process—from setting goals for learning, to collecting data, to considering with colleagues how findings may be used to guide improvement.

- Encouraging faculty and student affairs professionals to use assessment information requires implementation of a variety of creative dissemination strategies.

More recent columns foreshadow what many of us hope for the future of outcomes assessment, that is, that more scholars will contribute to the growing literature of assessment and thus push the field forward. In 2006 I described the first large-scale study that demonstrates the power of assessment in increasing student learning when applied purposefully in the process of curriculum change.

You Won't Find This in Books

Since 1989 I have participated in a book project almost every year, sometimes as a coauthor but more often as the editor of a collection of works contributed by others. (My own scholarship clearly fits in the category Ernest Boyer [1990] called integration.) From time to time I couldn't resist taking advantage of the bully pulpit I've enjoyed as the editor of *Assessment Update* to share some perspectives I'd developed, or some examples of good practice I'd encountered, as a result of my experiences in preparing a new book manuscript.

Three questions guided the development of my first major book, *Making a Difference: Outcomes of a Decade of Assessment in Higher Education* (Banta & Associates, 1993). I wanted to know if faculty were teaching more effectively, if students were learning more, and if the quality of colleges and universities was improving as a result of widespread use of outcomes assessment. Each of three "Editor's Notes" columns addressed one of those questions, and the column focused on institutional quality is included here.

In 2002 almost two dozen colleagues contributed chapters to the book *Building a Scholarship of Assessment* (Banta & Associates, 2002). I remember arguing with the editors at Jossey-Bass about the title because I wanted to convey the idea that this branch of scholarship was just beginning to emerge and that this would not be the (my?) last, and certainly not the definitive, book on this subject. I insisted that we not call the work simply

"Scholarship of Assessment," and at length we agreed that adding the word 'building' to the title would accommodate my desire to signal that we were, and still are, at an early stage in the development of this literature. In my 2002 column in this section I identify Alverno College and James Madison University as two institutions where "systematic inquiry designed to deepen and extend the foundation of knowledge underlying our field" (my words from that column) is under way.

In 2005 I conducted telephone interviews with eleven top administrators at a national sample of colleges and universities where distinctive assessment programs had helped to transform those institutions. My 2006 column in this section contains descriptions of some of the assessment methods these leaders had found particularly effective.

Designing Effective Assessment: Principles and Profiles of Good Practice (Banta, Jones, and Black, 2009) was based on a national search for examples of effective practice in outcomes assessment. In my 2009 column herein I lament the fact that only 9 (6%) of the 146 institutional profiles we received for this book contain evidence that student learning has improved over time as a result of assessing learning and using the findings to improve instruction, curriculum, or academic support services such as advising.

One Bird's-Eye View of the U.S. Landscape for Assessment

My involvement in outcomes assessment, which stems from my preparation and experience in measurement and program evaluation, began in 1980 when I was asked to assist in developing the University of Tennessee, Knoxville (UTK) response to the performance funding initiative of the Tennessee Higher Education Commission. With assistance provided by multiyear grants obtained in 1985, 1988, and 1989, I established the Center for Assessment Research and Development at UTK. And of course I have served as editor of *Assessment Update* since 1989. Accordingly I have been invited to participate in a number of national projects focused, broadly speaking, on outcomes assessment.

In 1990 President George H. W. Bush, his secretary of education, Lamar Alexander, and the nation's governors agreed on six national goals for education as the bases for *America 2000*, a program aimed at educational improvement and achievement of the six goals. Goal 5, Objective 5 stated that by 2000 "the proportion of college graduates who demonstrate an advanced ability to think critically, communicate effectively, and solve problems will increase substantially." Those last two words implied that the named skills would be measured somehow. And that implication led to an intense effort on the part of the National Center for Education Statistics (NCES) between 1990 and 1995 to make plans to develop a standardized test for the three skills that could be administered to college seniors. Early in that period I was one of fifteen individuals invited to prepare position papers to provide direction for the development of the national test. My 1992, 1993, and 1996 columns in this section contain my recollections of the attempt to build support for the national test.

The 1994 Congress was swept into office with a presumed mandate to carry out the "Contract for America," and funding the construction of a national test for college students was not in the contract. Sal Corallo, the chief architect of the NCES effort to build the national test, retired, and for nearly a decade the notion of improving America's colleges and universities by testing their students lay dormant.

The press to assess with a test sprang to life again with the issuance in 2006 of the report of Secretary of Education Margaret Spelling's Commission on the Future of Higher Education. That report called for measures of the value added by colleges and universities and publicly reported scores on standardized tests that would permit comparison of institutional quality. Two large national associations, the American Association of State Colleges and Universities (AASCU) and the National Association of State Universities and Land Grant Colleges (NASULGC), came together to head off any efforts by the U.S. Department of Education to impose national measures of institutional quality, including a national test.

When my colleague Gary Pike and I were conducting research on the technical qualities of standardized tests of generic skills at UTK, little did we know that ours would remain the only large-scale studies of their kind for the next 25 years. So we were somewhat surprised to find ourselves appointed to two of the working groups that AASCU and NASULGC administrators asked to develop what came to be called the Voluntary System of Accountability (VSA). In my 2008 column herein I describe the concerns about currently available standardized tests of generic skills that we raised as a result of our studies in Tennessee. I also reveal that my objections to including a measure of value added based on test scores as a non-negotiable component of the VSA were overruled by other members of my working group.

In my 2010 column herein I raise a new concern: Assessment designed to address accountability demands—that is, using standardized test scores and value-added measures to compare the quality of institutions—may actually damage our years of work to make outcomes assessment serve to guide institutional improvement efforts. I describe promising new work with authentic measures such as electronic portfolios and rubrics, but I raise measurement-related cautions about these measures as well.·

Tripping Lightly Around the Globe

I must begin this section by emphasizing that I have not developed deep knowledge of any national system of assessment, or quality assurance as it is called elsewhere, other than that of the United States. I have been invited to speak and/or consult in a number of countries, and I have tried to study quality assurance/assessment (QA) in those countries in preparing for my assignments. Then I have been able to observe their QA initiatives first-hand during my brief visits. But most of my written observations about assessment in other countries are based on conversing with colleagues and listening to presentations while attending an average of two overseas professional meetings each year since the late 1980s. Between 1989 and 2003, on behalf of my university I co-sponsored with academic partners in England and Scotland fifteen international conferences on assessing quality in higher education. And almost every year since 1990 I have participated in the annual meeting of the European Association for Institutional Research (EAIR).

At the first international conference co-sponsored by my university (UTK), which was held at Cambridge University in England, the 45 participants from 9 countries were so often confused by terms like course (meaning course of study in England and a single component of a degree program in the U.S.) that they recommended developing a glossary of such terms. Aided by the glossary we had prepared in the interim, the 80 participants from 20 countries who attended the second conference in the series at St. Andrews University in Scotland were ready to engage in spirited discussions of government QA policies and faculty reactions to them. My 1990 column provides some highlights of the presentations by colleagues from Germany, England, the Netherlands, and Mexico.

In a 1992 column I describe the new interest in using student evaluations and peer review to assess and improve quality in German universities. These observations were gleaned from the experience of participating as an invited presenter at a meeting in Bonn in February 1992 that was sponsored by the German Federal Ministry for Education and Science.

By 1994, the date of the third column in this section, the international conference series that I had started while at UTK was cosponsored by my new institution, Indiana University-Purdue University Indianapolis. The Sixth International Conference on Assessing Quality in Higher Education (AQHE) was held in Hong Kong, and attracted participants from 28 countries, including Australia, China, Japan, South Africa, and Taiwan. Delegates from the Asian countries were particularly enthusiastic about applying Total Quality Management (TQM) and ISO 9000 quality audits in their universities. Performance funding experiments were reportedly under way in Australia and Scotland, and delegates from Chile, along with those from several European countries, presented papers on the search for national performance indicators.

In my 1999 column I note that for the first time there were delegates from Nepal, India, Nigeria, Botswana, and Kenya, as well as several historically black universities in South Africa, at our eleventh AQHE conference in Manchester, England. Conversations in special interest groups on teaching and learning, faculty development, institutional effectiveness, workforce and vocational education, TQM, and QA policy were more intense and lively than ever. Emphasizing the commonality of QA interests worldwide, papers on assessment in general education, major fields, and institutional effectiveness were offered by delegates from several other countries in addition to the U.S.

In 2002 I contrasted the themes of two conferences: "The End of Quality" for one held in England and "How can we use assessment to improve teaching and learning?" for one in the U.S. I speculated that the difference in perspectives might have something to do with the fact that central governments in the United Kingdom and Europe play a much larger role in regulating and monitoring universities than is the case in the U.S. Thus participants in the British conference were voicing their worries that the government's heavy hand in conducting external quality reviews was actually having a detrimental effect on tertiary education.

My 2009 column brings us to the current scene. The title, "Sour Notes from Europe," is a too-obvious play on the term *tuning*, the process of encouraging academics in a given discipline to develop common student learning outcomes that will guide instruction across universities and across national boundaries. While tuning began as an initiative of the European Union, the Lumina Foundation is supporting tuning projects in this country. At the 2009 EAIR meeting in Vilnius, Lithuania, that I attended, several presenters described the dangers of narrowing curriculum that they see associated with specifying common learning outcomes. Moreover, the secretary general of the European University Association asserted that the Bologna Process, of which tuning is a component, has created as much diversity—profile building, branding, competition—among European universities as it has produced subject-specific convergence.

I conclude that 2009 column on a positive note, as I will here. The best session I attended in Lithuania was one in which four undergraduate psychology majors from the University of Freiburg in Germany described their use of community-organizing techniques to attract faculty attention to their concerns about the effects of the Bologna Process on students. One of the groups they organized wrote student learning outcomes and Freiburg faculty are adopting those! Perhaps it is our students who ultimately will be successful in engaging more of our faculty colleagues in using outcomes assessment to improve teaching and learning.

References

Banta, T. W. & Associates. (2002). *Building a Scholarship of Assessment*. San Francisco, CA: Jossey-Bass.

Banta, T. W. & Associates. (1993). *Making a Difference: Outcomes of a Decade of Assessment in Higher Education*. San Francisco, CA: Jossey-Bass.

Banta, T. W., Jones, E. A., & Black, K. E. (2009). *Designing Effective Assessment: Principles and Profiles of Good Practice*. San Francisco, CA: Jossey-Bass.

Boyer, E. L. (1990). *Scholarship Reconsidered: Priorities of the Professoriate*. Princeton, NJ: Carnegie.

Ewell, P. T. (1984). *The Self-Regarding Institution*. Boulder, CO: National Center for Higher Education Management Systems.

Some Things Never Change

On the Crest of the Wave

Look for the genesis of Assessment Update *and an overview of the assessment scene in Spring 1989. From* Assessment Update *1:1 (1989).*

Response to the idea of publishing a newsletter on assessment in higher education has been immediate, strong, and positive. Last fall Jossey-Bass sent out a questionnaire designed to test the waters for a newsletter. Within a few weeks, over a third of the questionnaires came back, all supporting the concept, with most containing content suggestions and offers to contribute information.

We hope you will follow through with those offers. Since we don't have reporters strategically stationed around the globe, we will depend on our readers to send us the news. Articles of any length (up to 3,000 words) will be welcome. Send us announcements of meetings to come, reviews of meetings just held, word of collaborative efforts, insights about how assessment works (or doesn't work), stories about innovative assessment activities, and any other relevant information. Please direct your contributions to: Editor, *Assessment Update*, Assessment Resource Center, 2046 Terrace Avenue, Knoxville, TN 37996-3504.

Last June, Gale Erlandson, higher education editor at Jossey-Bass Publishers, asked if I would serve as editor for a newsletter on assessment. It would be an entirely new venture for Jossey-Bass—its first newsletter—as well as for me, but both Gale and I felt this type of publication was exactly right for keeping up with a burgeoning and rapidly chang-ing field. Always-supportive administrators at UTK promised assistance. Longtime friends Peter Ewell, Pat Hutchings, Gary Pike, Marcia Ment-kowski, and John Harris pledged their support. And more recent ac-quaintances Peter Gray and Larry Braskamp offered specific, immediate help. How could anyone say no in light of such enthusiasm? I promise that with your help and that of our consulting editors, we will try to report on the most promising practices and the most timely issues in assessment.

Having Peter Ewell as author of the lead article is a special treat. Since we met in 1982, Peter and I have been sharing our perceptions about assessment wherever we meet—in airports, at receptions, in deans' offices, speeding to the next appointment in a rented car. In 1986 we began to ask each other, "Has the assessment wave crested?" Each suc-ceeding year we have admitted, with some incredulity, that interest has continued to grow. Peter's theme "about halfway" expresses well the feel-ing many of us have about our position in the history of assessment in higher education.

Most faculty, especially those in the nation's largest institutions, are just starting to hear the roar of the first waves of assessment hitting the shore. Two-thirds of the states and all six regional accrediting agencies have taken some action to stimulate institutional interest in the assess-ment of outcomes. On July 1, 1988, the *Federal Register* published the final regulations for the Secretary of Education's "Procedures and Criteria for Recognition of Accrediting Agencies." The regulations include: a section called "Focus on Educational Effectiveness," which specifies that each ac-crediting agency must determine whether or not an institution or program (1) maintains clearly specified educational objectives consistent with its mission; (2) documents the educational achievements of its students "in verifiable and consistent ways," such as evaluation of senior theses, stan-dardized test results, and employer evaluations; (3) publicizes for the ben-efit of prospective students its educational objectives and the results of its assessment procedures; and (4) systematically applies the information obtained through assessment "to foster enhanced student achievement."

The pervasive nature of the state mandates and accreditation criteria, as well as the genuine desire to promote student development, brought faculty all over the country together for state and regional meetings during the fall of 1988. At the annual meetings of the American Evaluation Association and the American Educational Research Association, sessions on assessment in higher education were added to the agendas; this indicates that assessment practitioners are building bridges to the research communities with which this fledgling field must be linked.

Interest in assessment is growing internationally. In 1986 UTK and Northeast Missouri State University were invited to make presentations in Paris at a meeting of the Organization for Economic Cooperation and Development. Faculty at Alverno College have made several presentations in England and Europe. In 1987 the first Sino-American Symposium on Program Evaluation in Higher Education was held at Peking University. This June a second team of American assessment specialists will travel to Beijing for five days of presentations and dialogue with faculty from thirty or more Chinese universities. On July 24–27, UTK will cosponsor an international conference on assessment to be held at Cambridge University. Conferees will consider the feasibility of international collaboration on matters related to assessment.

We hope to keep you apprised of future developments in assessment through feature articles, short perspectives pieces, news items, a resource column, a calendar of coming events, and continuing features on state initiatives, campus programs, and assessment instruments. This launch issue was assembled several months prior to publication; however, more short pieces and more news are planned for future issues. If you have additional suggestions for the presentation of content, please send them to us.

———————

Weaving Assessment into the Fabric of Higher Education

Look for a brief description of the powerful influence outcomes assessment had on three institutions considered pioneers in implementing assessment. In 1989, at Alverno College, Northeast Missouri State University, and the University of Tennessee, Knoxville, assessment was an integral part of some daily activities that faculty and administrators valued. From Assessment Update *1:2 (1989).*

With most people in higher education now aware of assessment, the movement has entered an intensive implementation phase. Experimentation with a variety of methods is taking place. A few institutions have moved with their assessment efforts into the phase of the change process known as *institutionalization*. Assessment leaders with programs at this stage of development are arguing strongly that assessment should be incorporated into such established institutional practices as planning, student development programming, and comprehensive academic program review.

Critics have expressed the hope that assessment will not command as much attention in the future as it has in the past four years, because it has "overshadowed many of the other critical issues facing higher education." I believe this view implies the failure to recognize the positive role that assessment can play in helping to achieve these and other important goals, if it is firmly woven into the institutional tapestry.

At pioneering institutions like Alverno College and Northeast Missouri University, early assessment initiatives created unique campus identities that began to attract outstanding students and faculty. Since then, Alverno has based an entire undergraduate curriculum on closely monitored development of individual students, an approach that has brought opportunities for external funding and for sharing methods with other institutions that hope to duplicate Alverno's successes (see Stone and Meyer, 1989, in Resources). In its second decade of assessment, Northeast used a sophisticated knowledge base, derived from assessment, to plan its transformation from one of several regional universities into Missouri's only liberal arts institution.

In 1983, on my own campus, assessment was made a component of a strong nine-year-old program review process. Recently, one of the University of Tennessee, Knoxville, humanities departments produced an exemplary self-study, which made good use of data we provide from surveys of faculty, undergraduates, and graduate students, information that our assessment office provides. The self-study process fostered consensus among the faculty about program strengths and weaknesses and future directions for the department. External reviewers were able to reach conclusions early in their campus visit and then to concentrate on the details of making recommendations for departmental improvements that will be considered and acted on by the faculty and by the departmental, college, and university administrators.

Colleges that engage in rational planning—specifying objectives for student development; implementing curricula, methods of instruction, and campus services to accomplish these ends with students; and using assessment results to chart progress and make warranted improvements—can secure the future of assessment, because it will be such an integral part of our day-to-day activities. Moreover, assessment will not be viewed as a competing demand for attention if it is considered a means to effect improvement in every institutional process.

Revealing the Results of Assessment

Look for a variety of ways to disseminate findings and communicate the importance of assessment on a campus. From Assessment Update 3:3 (1991).

As campus assessment coordinator at the University of Tennessee, Knoxville (UTK), I spend a great deal of my time communicating the results of assessment to various campus audiences. I believe that this activity is among the most important of my responsibilities because even the most significant findings may go virtually unnoticed if no one points them out to those who could use them.

We begin each academic year by distributing to the academic affairs staff and deans a volume we call the *Detailed Summary of Instructional Evaluation Data*. It includes a one- or two-page synopsis of the findings of each of the major data-gathering activities we conducted as part of the assessment program during the previous year. The 1990 volume contains the results of testing seniors in general education and in selected major fields, of reviewing several master's degree programs, and of surveying samples of freshmen, enrolled undergraduates, undergraduate dropouts, seniors, and alumni.

In October 1990, we inaugurated an assessment column in the bi-weekly newspaper distributed to all faculty and staff. This provides an opportunity for broader distribution of some of the findings in the *Detailed Summary*.

Over the years, we have tried to tailor the content of our data-collection strategies to reflect many of the broad goals contained in college- and university-wide planning documents. Annually, we develop a report for the deans and the Planning Committee that provides evidence of progress in meeting the relevant goals. For instance, as a research university, we worry so much about students' access to faculty that we have made "to increase faculty-student interaction" one of our institutional goals. As evidence of progress in this direction, in 1983 a survey of undergraduates revealed that 49% knew no faculty members well enough to ask for recommendations; by 1990, this percentage had fallen to 27%.

Periodically, faculty and/or staff committees are appointed to study particular issues, such as student retention, the experience of older students, women's concerns, or campus library resources. With our survey responses, we have recorded sufficient background information to be able to fashion special reports for these groups. One finding was of particular interest to the library committee: as a result of the opening of a new facility in 1988, students' library use—occasional or frequent—rose, from 53% in 1983 to 90% by 1990. These special reports also have proved helpful to departments, colleges, and the university in providing concrete evidence for accrediting agencies of effectiveness in meeting specified goals.

By far the most effective channel for communicating assessment results at UTK has been the comprehensive program-review process.

Peer review is taken very seriously at UTK. One year before a visit by peers, faculty in a department begin to develop a self-study that outlines goals, curricula, and perceived strengths and weaknesses. Two outside specialists in the discipline are joined by three UTK reviewers outside the department for a visit of two-and-a-half days. The visit includes interviews with virtually everyone associated with the program, from the chancellor and his staff to faculty and students and even heads of related departments. Reviewers provide written recommendations, and departmental faculty consider these and develop a written response that becomes the object of consideration at a follow-up meeting, which involves the responsible dean and appropriate representatives of the central administration. All concerned officials eventually sign an agreement specifying how each one will help the department carry out the actions necessary to address the recommendations considered most important. In a recent, almost extraordinary, attempt to ensure follow-up action, UTK has instituted a midcycle review. Full-scale reviews take place every eight years, but during the fourth year between these reviews, one of the outside reviewers is brought back to conduct, along with the three UTK reviewers, a visit of a day-and-a-half, which once again brings the attention of the chancellor and his staff, the dean, and the department to the business of responding to the earlier recommendations for strengthening the department.

In 1983, we added to the guidelines for the departmental self-study the section "Evidence of Program Effectiveness." Prior to 1983, the guidelines had asked the department to describe its resources and processes for achieving goals, but not its goal-related outcomes.

Also in 1983, my office began to collect assessment evidence for each department, evidence that could be included in its self-study—general education and disciplinary testing results, with appropriate comparative data, and targeted survey responses obtained from students, faculty, and alumni. We provide detailed reports for perusal by departmental faculty as well as brief summaries that can be included without modification, if desired, in the self-study document. This information can enhance faculty's and reviewers' understanding of the extent to which the department is achieving its stated goals.

Revealing the results of assessment to faculty at the time of program review has proved to be the mode of communication most likely to produce lasting change at UTK. Departments have given increased attention to internships, become more active in placing graduates, revamped introductory courses, instituted departmental newsletters, and even changed curricula as assessment data have focused the attention of faculty and reviewers on areas in need of improvement. This internal use of data in the formative evaluation of academic units is perhaps the most significant contribution that assessment has to make in higher education.

This One's for Students

Look for examples of faculty collecting information about the experiences of students and using that to improve instruction. From Assessment Update *7:3 (1995).*

With great pleasure we present an issue in which the spotlight is squarely on students. Since our readers as well as our contributors are principally college and university faculty and administrators, *Assessment Update* is always filled with articles designed to help faculty understand and improve assessment practice. In this regard, this issue is no exception; the articles will enrich faculty perspectives. The difference is that instead of the usual focus of faculty writing about and learning from the experience of faculty colleagues, most of the articles herein describe ways in which faculty can learn by tapping the experience of students.

Nearing the midpoint of our seventh year of editing *Assessment Update*, I can look back and find only one previous issue in which the cover article featured students as key players in assessment: Douglas Lee Hall of St. Mary's University in San Antonio gave us the wonderful story "Involving Students as Active Participants in Assessment" (*Assessment Update*, 1993, 5(5), 1–2,6). As the new, overworked chair of computer sciences, Hall gratefully accepted an offer of help from his college work-study student. He asked her to assist him in thinking through the curriculum for a new bachelor of science degree that the faculty intended to propose. This experience was so positive that Hall asked his colleagues to nominate representatives for a computer science advisory board, to be made up solely of students. Using Association for Computing Machinery guidelines, the students developed a proposal for the new undergraduate curriculum that included rationales for all of the courses as well as for their sequencing. The department's faculty accepted the proposal with little change, and the university's academic council approved it with comments about "how well the curriculum had been thought out, how rigorous it was, and how reflective it was of the purpose and mission of the university" (Hall, 1993, p. 1).

The majority of articles in this issue of *Assessment Update* attest the value for faculty of involving students in assessment. The lead article is the first in a series of four reports on the use of Total Quality Management (TQM), or Continuous Quality Improvement (CQI), in higher education. Judy Griffith, John McLure, and Jann Weitzel take on one of the most vexing challenges to faculty—the large class—and show how they have used TQM strategies to improve the student experience in a required teacher education course at the University of Iowa. For instance, a color-coded seating chart that includes some information about each student has helped make learning more personal, discussions more interesting, and classroom participation more universal. A simple knowledge checklist asks students to rate on a three-point scale their knowledge of important concepts that the course is designed to cover. The results enable the instructors to assign meaningful readings and to skim over certain concepts in order to spend more time on others. Assessment of written work with detailed marginal comments helps students improve their grades on papers and midterm exams if they are willing to revise their originals and resubmit them.

Speaking with the authority of a professor in the School of Business at the University of Indianapolis, Leslie Gardner observes in the second article that "efficiency is increased by eliminating the need for a separate time slot for a classroom assessment activity by combining that activity with the teaching of process improvement." Students spend some of their class time in groups of three or four, applying to the task of improving the class the CQI techniques of brainstorming, prioritizing ideas, constructing Pareto charts and fishbone diagrams, and conducting surveys. Students are graded on completion of a prescribed sequence of CQI activities and on the practicality of implementing the improvements they have suggested.

In team teaching a TQM course at Marietta College, Alice M. Warner and David Cress tossed aside the syllabus, text, and traditional methods of assessment and engaged in collaborative efforts with their students to design the course and appropriate assessment techniques. Both instructors and students developed portfolios that included individual and group learning goals, papers reflecting on processes and progress, class improvement feedback sheets completed at the end of each class, and concrete evidence that learning was taking place. An important aspect of the learning that occurred was public sharing of the personal evaluations as they were added to the portfolios. The instructors' reflection papers were particularly important to the students' understanding of how relationships with peers can enhance the learning of individuals.

The article by Paula M. Rooney and P. Gerard Shaw illustrates the increasingly popular CQI practice of benchmarking. When registration and the billing process topped the list of campus irritants in student surveys conducted at Babson College in 1989 and again in 1993, the Babson student affairs staff began looking for a college or university that had solved its registration problems. When they could not find good models in higher education, Babson staff turned to their food service provider, the Marriott Corporation. They found that Marriott's hotel affiliate had been working for years to improve its registration process, and that Marriott could provide benchmarks for Babson in this area. Using technology, Babson now handles most of the registration process by mail and telephone, thus eliminating waiting lines and "saving paper, time, and money." Continuous assessment of student opinion will enable Babson to tell if the improvements are satisfying its customers.

Joe V. Chandler and Bettie Home report on the use of a particularly comprehensive set of questions in exit interviews for students in the Division of Physical Education and Exercise Studies at Lander University. Not only do the interviews solicit opinions about campus programs and services but they also ask about the strengths and weaknesses of the university's general education program and about the teaching effectiveness of individual professors in the division. At the end of the interview, the questioner—always someone from outside the division—rates the student's verbal communication skills. Students' complaints about the difficulty of scheduling certain courses convinced faculty to teach most courses annually as opposed to every other year, two courses thought to contain needless overlap were revised, and some negative evaluations shared privately by the division chair with a single professor led that individual to make changes in teaching methods.

Dennis E. Peacock gives us an early report on a campuswide student advisory group at Northeast Missouri State University that helps "assess assessment." In its first year this body has worked to improve (1) the design, content, and return rate of student surveys; (2) the interpretation of survey findings and general education test scores; and (3) students' motivation to do their best work on the general education exams.

In a relatively new field like outcomes assessment, it is important for faculty to talk first among themselves about useful materials and techniques. The majority of articles here argue strongly for involving students in the conversation as soon as possible. Faculty know most about course content—*what* students should learn—but students know most about *how* they learn. They can tell us much about the teaching strategies that help them grasp the important content most efficiently and effectively. We can improve our practice by listening to them.

———————————

The Power of a Matrix

Look for examples of using a matrix to organize thinking about how to approach outcomes assessment in a variety of contexts. From Assessment Update 8:4 (1996).

Recent experiences at Iowa State University and on my own campus have convinced me to write about a tentative conclusion I reached about four years ago. I have come to believe that a simple matrix can be a powerful tool for helping faculty plan and organize an approach to assessment. Even a concept as abstract and complex as assessment can be made more concrete and comprehensible as relationships among its component parts are depicted visually in a single graphic image.

A faculty committee with responsibility for assessment at Iowa State used a matrix to enable department faculty to conceptualize assessment of student learning in the major. At Indiana University-Purdue University Indianapolis (IUPUI), general education is the current focus of a series of matrices developed to guide our work. Drawing on these experiences, I construct examples here to illustrate how the use of matrices can assist in planning for assessment with respect to both the major and general education.

The matrix is a versatile construction. It can be very simple or quite complex, ranging from a single element tracked over two dimensions (a 1-by-2 matrix), to two elements with two dimensions each (a 2-by-2 matrix), to many elements with many dimensions (X-by-Y matrix).

An excellent way to begin any faculty discussion of assessment is to ask what students should know and be able to do when they complete a course of study. Such a conversation might produce a list such as the following: (1) write effectively, (2) speak persuasively, (3) manage time, (4) use a computer to acquire new information in the discipline, and (5) demonstrate the ability to apply theory in a practical context.

The next step might involve creating a 1-by-1 matrix for each of the five skills in which the skill is broken into a set of subskills. Table 1

Table 1. Skill-by Subskills Matrix

Skill	Subskills		
Time management	Manages own time	Manages one patient's care in specified time	Manages care of several patients in specified time
	Courses 101, 120	Clinical experience	Hospital setting

Table 2. Skill-by Courses Matrix

Skill	Courses		
	Course 101	Course 201	Course 401
Time management	Manages own time	Manages one patient's care in specified tim	Manages care of several patients in specified time

contains an analysis of the time management skill as conceptualized by the faculty of the Indiana University School of Nursing. Within the cells of this matrix, the nursing faculty have indicated the courses or other experiences in which students will be expected to develop the subskills they have identified. A variation on the skill-by-subskills matrix is the skill-by-courses matrix in Table 2.

Either of the simple matrices just described could be made more comprehensive by adding dimensions. Continuing with the five-skills example, a 5-by-X matrix could be developed to illustrate the critical skills and subskills all students are expected to develop by the time of graduation, along with the courses and other experiences that are designed to help students learn these skills.

Next comes the measurement question: What evidence do we need to convince us that students have learned the skills and knowledge we deem critical? Here a multidimensional subskills-by-measures matrix such as Table 3 can be helpful.

The rows of Table 3 assure us that we have multiple measures of each of the subskills; the credibility of our evidence is enhanced if it comes from several sources. The columns of Table 3 indicate the specific kinds

Table 3. Subskills-by-Measures Matrix

Subskills	Measures				
	Student Self-Assessment	Faculty Rating Scale	Supervisor Observation	Written Exam	Patient Questionnaire
Manages own time	✓	✓			
Manages one patient's care in specified time	✓		✓		
Manages care of several patients in specified time	✓		✓	✓	✓

of information each measure must contain if it is to fulfill its role in the assessment plan. For instance, in a self-assessment instrument designed for student use, we should include items that ask students if they feel confident that they can manage their own time, care for a single patient, and care for several patients effectively; then they might be asked if their program of study has contributed much or little to their expressed levels of confidence.

Most faculty want to know how they will find the extra time they believe will be needed to do the kind of comprehensive assessment of student learning that external demands for accountability require. The use of matrices can help faculty see that they are already collecting in their own courses much of the evidence needed for credible, comprehensive assessment. Moreover, the faculty development that occurs during conversations about assessment prompted by matrix construction can lead to improvements in course and curriculum structure and in pedagogy that make faculty work not only more effective but also more efficient, thus saving time in the long run. Combining the information in a skills-by-courses matrix with that in a subskills-by-measures matrix (see Tables 2 and 3) can show not only where skills are to be taught but also where they can be assessed. Periodically, a faculty committee overseeing the comprehensive assessment of students' knowledge and skills can look at samples of student work that have already been evaluated for purposes of giving grades and reassess these samples to derive a general sense of whether most students are developing given skills at the level or levels that faculty find acceptable for program graduates. (Incidentally, the interest in looking across students and across courses to assess student development in a generic sense suggests the need for yet another type of matrix: the skills-by-standards for judgment matrix in which excellent, good, fair, and poor [for example] levels of performance for each skill are carefully described.)

The skills-by-process matrix developed by faculty at Iowa State University is a very effective tool for tracking progress in assessment at department and campus levels. In column 1, a department lists its desired learning outcomes for students; in column 2, the courses and other experiences where the outcomes are taught are specified; column 3 contains the measures associated with each outcome; column 4 contains a summary of assessment findings; and, in column 5, faculty are asked what changes, if any, they have undertaken in response to the findings.

Looking at the five-column matrix constructed by each of Iowa State's departments, we can see many of the benefits that a conscientious approach to outcomes assessment confers. Bringing faculty together for collective consideration of desired student learning outcomes produces a better understanding by faculty and students of the role each course can and should play in overall student development. This understanding can create better focus in teaching, more deliberate sequencing of concepts, and thus improved learning. If students and graduates, employers, and other community representatives are involved in the goal-setting process, the experience can be even richer and the outcomes even more relevant, current, and motivating for students.

Consideration of tools and methods for assessment of comprehensive student outcomes can help faculty learn more about setting criteria for judgment and developing more valid assessment methods for use in their own courses. Once again, this activity can be enriched by the involvement of students, graduates, employers, and others. Students can tell us how questions should be worded to communicate the intended meaning. Those outside the academy can suggest assessment activities and contexts and even participate as assessors.

Finally, in addition to making constructive contributions to curriculum development, course sequencing, pedagogy, and assessment, matrices can help to improve student advising. The skill-by-subskill and skill-by-courses matrices can be used in orientation and subsequent advising sessions to help students visualize the curriculum and understand what they are expected to know and be able to do as they progress. With the addition of the skills-by-measures matrix, students learn when and how their achievement will be assessed. Having these blueprints should help students develop a better sense of purpose and thus become more highly motivated.

Iowa State's five-dimensional matrix focuses attention on the long-range and iterative nature of assessment: Measures yield findings that call for responsive actions, which, in turn, suggest revisions in desired learning outcomes. Thus, the use of a matrix series can produce improvements in current practice that continue to benefit students and faculty in a continuous cycle of improvements.

Welcome News About the Impact of Assessment

Look for a brief history of outcomes assessment from 1979 to 2006 and a summary of the first large-scale study demonstrating that assessment can play an important role in increasing student learning. From Assessment Update 18:5 (2006).

As a member of the closing panel at the assessment conference sponsored by the National Association of Student Personnel Administrators in Phoenix, Arizona, in June, I heard from the moderator that oft-repeated question: What impact has assessment had on higher education? That question has always troubled me—for two reasons. First, we have tried to say over and over that assessment cannot and should not stand alone. It is a process designed to promote continual improvement that should be embedded in our goals and plans for student learning in particular and for higher education in general. Thus, the impact of assessment cannot be separated from the impact of other powerful forces shaping higher education today.

The second reason I find it troubling to be asked about the impact of assessment is that in all the years since 1979, when Tennessee became the first state to implement a true performance funding scheme for public colleges and universities, we have not been successful in demonstrating the accountability of higher education to our external stakeholders. Governors, legislators, and other community leaders have asked us over and over to give them some easily understood metrics that would enable them to compare the effectiveness of diverse institutions, and we have not been able to satisfy them in this regard.

Despite my reservations about it, the question about the impact of assessment is a fair one, and one we will continue to hear. In my response in Phoenix, I focused on the interdependence of assessment and many of the other important movements that have influenced higher education over the last quarter century. I believe that the collective impact of these forces has been to increase colleges' and universities' focus on students and on the effects of their college experiences on their learning.

First came the accountability movement. In the early 1980s, the competition for increasingly scarce public funds among various social services—health care for the disadvantaged, highways, prisons, public schools—ensured that higher education would have to do a better job of demonstrating value for tax dollars spent. By 1985, Tennessee had been joined by Virginia, New Jersey, and Colorado in enacting mandates for colleges and universities to demonstrate student learning. Tennessee's approach was the most prescriptive, specifying, among other things, that graduating seniors would take a given standardized test in general education and that the same questionnaire would be administered to graduates of all institutions so that mean institutional responses on each item could be calculated and compared across all public institutions in the state. The age of assessment had dawned.

In 1987, the Wingspread Principles for Good Practice in Undergraduate Learning (Chickering and Gamson, 1987) were formulated by a group of scholars devoted to research on college student learning. These leaders said, in effect, that while we await development of reliable and valid ways to measure college student learning directly, we can substitute some indirect, proxy measures of learning based on research showing that engaged students learn more. That is, if we can demonstrate that students are spending more time studying, interacting with faculty on matters of intellectual substance, working on projects with peers, and engaging actively in their learning, we can infer that they are learning more. The Wingspread principles have provided the basis for a number of contemporary assessment instruments, including the National Survey of Student Engagement.

By 1990, the total quality management movement that had influenced the behavior of American corporations in the 1980s was being adapted for application in higher education. It was quickly renamed *continuous quality improvement* in colleges and universities. Assessment is a vital component of the plan-do-check (or assess)-act cycle that enables continuous improvement of processes in higher education.

The 1990s brought us two more powerful movements that increased the focus on students and incorporated assessment in their implementation. Barr and Tagg (1995) wrote a compelling essay that called on academics to change the focus of their attention from what they teach to what students are learning. Boyer (1990) elevated the stature of the scholarship of teaching as compared with the scholarship of discovery (basic research). Subsequently, the scholarship of teaching became the scholarship of teaching and learning (SoTL), and SoTL groups have sprung up on college and university campuses across the land. Both of these movements require assessment to demonstrate the changes in student learning that their adherents seek.

Finally, the years since 1979 have brought substantive changes in regional and disciplinary accreditation processes. Influenced by all the forces just described, accreditors have shifted their sights from descriptions of the curricula and courses that faculty provide to the learning that students experience as an outcome of faculty efforts. Again, assessment provides the essential evidence that accreditors seek.

Mentioning accreditation brings me to the most important part of my response at the conference in Phoenix. Thanks to the Accreditation Board for Engineering and Technology (ABET), we now have the first large-scale study that demonstrates clearly that assessment can increase student learning when combined with identification of specific student learning outcomes, development of faculty to use proven pedagogies to promote learning and assessment of these outcomes, and engagement of students so they will take an active part in their learning.

In 1996, ABET directors adopted a new set of standards—Engineering Criteria 2000, or EC2000—that were designed to shift the basis for accreditation of engineering and technology programs from what is taught to what is learned. In EC2000, eleven learning outcomes are specified, and university faculty must assess and demonstrate student achievement of each. Students are still expected to develop high levels of math, science, and technical skills, but EC2000 also emphasizes other skills such as communicating effectively; working in teams; solving unstructured problems; and demonstrating ethical behavior, awareness of global issues, and professionalism.

In 2002, ABET commissioned Lisa R. Lattuca, Patrick T. Terenzini, and J. Fredericks Volkwein of the Center for the Study of Higher Education at Pennsylvania State University to conduct an evaluation of the effects of EC2000. The resulting study, *Engineering Change: A Study of the Impact of EC2000* (Lattuca, Terenzini, and Volkwein, 2006), was completed in late 2005.

Lattuca, Terenzini, and Volkwein conducted a comprehensive study. Their findings are based on responses from 147 (of 203 contacted) engineering programs; 1,243 (of 2,971 surveyed) faculty; 39 (of 40 contacted) deans; 5,494 (of 13,054 contacted) 1994 graduates of the engineering programs responding (representing a cohort that graduated prior to implementation of EC2000); 4,330 (of 12,921 contacted) 2004 graduates of the 147 engineering programs (representing a post-EC2000 cohort); and 1,622 employers.

Faculty respondents to a questionnaire reported that while their emphasis on math, science, and technical skills had not diminished significantly, their focus on the new skills specified in EC2000 had increased substantially. Faculty also have engaged in more professional development activities and now use more active learning strategies such as computer simulations, case studies, and open-ended problems. Nearly 90 percent of respondents reported some personal effort in assessment.

In comparison with 1994 graduates, engineering graduates in 2004 reported more active engagement in their own learning, more interaction with their instructors, more faculty feedback on their work, more international travel, and more emphasis on openness to diverse people and ideas. (Note the basis in Wingspread principles.) In self-reports of their ability levels at the time of graduation, members of the class of 2004 rated themselves higher than did their 1994 peers not only on all of the new skills emphasized in EC2000, but also on basic math, science, and technical skills!

Employers' survey responses were a bit more mixed than those of faculty and graduates, but they generally confirmed the other findings. To employers, levels of math, science, and engineering skills among their employees appeared unchanged between 1994 and 2004, while modest increases were perceived in their employees' teamwork and communication skills, as well as their abilities to learn, grow, and adapt to changes in technologies and society. Employers perceived that modest declines had occurred over the decade in employees' problem-solving skills and understanding of the organizational, cultural, and environmental contexts and constraints of their work.

Lattuca, Terenzini, and Volkwein conclude their summary of findings with this statement: "As the first national study of an outcomes-based accreditation model, this research also informs ongoing discussions of accreditation policy among regional and professional accreditation agencies, state and federal legislators, and the general public—all of whom want evidence of the rigor of higher education quality assurance practices" (2006, p. 13). I would like to thank ABET and these scholars for giving us—at long last—this welcome evidence that assessment, in combination with a focus on specific learning outcomes, preparation of faculty to engage students in learning and to assess that learning, and consistent emphasis on assessment by an accreditor, can, in fact, increase student learning.

References

Barr, R. B., & Tagg, J. (1995). From Teaching to Learning: A New Paradigm for Undergraduate Education. *Change, 27*(6), 12–25.

Boyer, E. L. (1990). *Scholarship Reconsidered: Priorities of the Professoriate*. Princeton, NJ: Carnegie Foundation for the Advancement of Teaching.

Chickering, A., & Gamson, Z. (1987). Seven Principles for Good Practice in Undergraduate Education. *Wingspread Journal, 5*(2), 1–4.

Lattuca, L. R., Terenzini, P. T., & Volkwein, J. F. (2006). *Engineering Change: A Study of the Impact of EC2000*. Baltimore, MD: Accreditation Board for Engineering and Technology. Also available at http://www.abet.org/Linked%20Documents-UPDATE/White%20Papers/Engineering%20Change.pdf.

You Won't Find This in Books

Are We Making A Difference?

Look for descriptions of assessment initiatives at five institutions where strong leadership at the highest levels has helped assessment transform the institution. From Assessment Update *5:5 (1993).*

Darrell Krueger, who is now president of Winona State University, was once dean of instruction at Northeast Missouri State University. Charles McClain, then president of Northeast, used to ask repeatedly, "Darrell, are we making a difference?" In seeking the answer, Krueger and McClain embarked on a comprehensive program of student outcomes assessment that transformed Northeast. From a teacher's college with projections of declining enrollment, it became a thriving regional university. Ultimately it was designated as Missouri's liberal arts and science institution.

Last year I undertook a national study designed to respond to McClain's question for the field of assessment. We are well into our second decade of outcomes assessment in higher education. Has all of our activity—from state initiatives and accrediting requirements to assessment for improvement on campuses—made a difference? Are students learning more? Are faculty teaching more effectively? Are colleges and universities better? In this column, I will provide some information related to this last question. I'll address the others in future issues of *Assessment Update*.

I have collected data from well over 100 campuses where outcomes assessment has been under way for several years—long enough to make some difference. In looking at the examples of impact, it seems to me that they can be grouped into at least three categories: *institutions* where assessment has transformed the campus culture; campuswide assessment *programs* that have resulted in significant, though less pervasive, improvements; and assessment *techniques* that have produced positive changes in specific areas. I will try to characterize the influence of assessment at some of the "transformed" institutions in the paragraphs that follow.

More than twenty years ago, the faculty at Alverno College employed an extensive program of assessment of their graduates to help reshape the curriculum around eight basic abilities: communication, analysis, problem solving, valuing in decision making, interaction, global perspectives, effective citizenship, and aesthetic responsiveness. Since then Alverno faculty have developed ways to assess successive levels of these abilities in coursework, and their study of assessment has enabled them to improve course structure, teaching methods, and assessment techniques themselves. The quest of Alverno faculty for continuous improvement of student learning has enriched the understanding of faculty around the globe of such concepts as assessment as learning, contextual validity, portfolio assessment, assessment centers, and student self-assessment.

At Northeast Missouri, assessment was used initially to demonstrate that its graduates were "nationally competitive" in their chosen fields and that their experiences at Northeast had added value to their store of knowledge and skills. The university gradually acquired a national reputation for academic quality, which resulted in increases in both the number and the academic potential of students applying for admission. All these changes produced in the faculty at Northeast a sense of identity and pride in the institution that further transformed the university's culture.

Strong presidents—Sister Joel Read at Alverno and Charles Mc-Clain at Northeast Missouri—focused faculty attention on assessment at their institutions in the 1970s. In 1985, another president—Nathan Weiss at Kean College—launched his own crusade to stimulate faculty self-consciousness about the quality of student learning using outcomes assessment. Kean faculty developed their own definition of assessment and with it a sense of power and responsibility for setting the direction for individual programs. They worked with each other, with students, with alumni, and with employers to define goals and objectives for their programs, to develop assessment strategies, and to make appropriate improvements. Kean College now has evidence that the student experience is richer and that student satisfaction has increased.

Presidential leadership was also an essential factor in development of the Institutional Impact Project at Ohio University in 1980. Testing, surveys, and student tracking have helped direct numerous improvements in programs and services at that institution. Assessment evidence now shows that students' scores on national exams have increased, freshmen are more involved in the campus experience, faculty and students interact more, seniors are more satisfied, and freshman retention has improved.

At the University of Wisconsin, Superior, strong administrative and faculty leadership and an assessment grant from the Fund for the Improvement of Postsecondary Education transformed a troubled institution with dangerously low enrollment to today's institution with rising enrollments and a much-improved public image in its region. An assessment program that has helped to improve teaching, increase affective support for students, and raise levels of expectation and performance for students has produced more satisfied faculty, freshmen who report a more positive initial impression of the university, and students who find their classes more challenging.

Leaders at these transformed institutions have kept assessment at the forefront of everyone's thinking for years. Assessment has been accorded time to develop in an orderly way, with a clear purpose, with widespread participation by all who should be concerned about the education of students: faculty, students themselves, administrators, graduates, employers, and community members. All five institutions have strong and effective assessment coordinators, drawn most often from the faculty. Since these individuals had earned the respect of their colleagues before they were given their assessment roles, they have been able to steer the campus assessment strategies through the sometimes treacherous shoals of faculty scrutiny and skepticism.

At these institutions, assessment findings are widely disseminated in a trusting atmosphere; negative results are not used to punish students or faculty. Assessment on these campuses is firmly anchored in established procedures that faculty care about, such as institutional planning and budgeting, curriculum development, faculty and staff development, and faculty scholarship. This fact, coupled with careful,.persistent follow-up, has made assessment part of the fabric of these institutions and ensured its lasting influence.

The stories of assessment's impact on the five institutions just identified, as well as more than 100 others, have been collected in a book, *Making a Difference: Outcomes of a Decade of Assessment in Higher Education*, to be published by Jossey-Bass in October 1993. Because each chapter is written by the individuals who shepherded the assessment process being described, the volume has 45 coauthors. For the material I've just summarized, I'd like to thank the following authors: Georgine Loacker and Marcia Mentkowski at Alverno, Candace Young at Northeast Missouri, Michael Knight at Kean, Michael Williford and Gary Moden at Ohio University, and Albert Katz at University of Wisconsin, Superior.

Toward a Scholarship of Assessment

Look for distinctions between scholarly assessment and the scholarship of assessment and some suggestions for enhancing the latter. From Assessment Update *14:2 (2002).*

In the article featured on the first page of this issue, T. Dary Erwin and Christine DeMars ask, "But where is the discussion, particularly in the assessment community, about technologically delivered assessment? . . . Where are the innovations in computer-based testing?" Like many other colleagues in assessment, Erwin and DeMars are calling for more systematic inquiry designed to deepen and extend the foundation of knowledge underlying our field. Since 1999, the term *scholarship of assessment* has gained widespread attention and use as the descriptor for this work.

So what exactly is the scholarship of assessment? What are the established fields of inquiry that support this scholarship? Where is it under way? What has it taught us thus far? What are some of the most promising topics for assessment scholarship in the near future? These are the major questions addressed in the book *Building a Scholarship of Assessment* (Banta and Associates, forthcoming), which will be published in April 2002. The book's fifteen chapters include one by T. Dary Erwin and Steven Wise and others by Tom Angelo, Peter Ewell, Peter Gray, George Kuh, Marcia Mentkowski and Georgine Loacker, Catherine Palomba, Gary Pike, Marvin Peterson, and Barbara Wright, as well as additional chapters by still more scholars whose work in assessment is becoming recognized as holding great promise for advancing the future of the field.

Since assessment is a vital component of teaching, the scholarship of assessment is closely allied with the scholarship of teaching (Boyer, 1990). The scholarship of assessment is systematic inquiry that involves basing studies on relevant theory or practice, gathering evidence, developing a summary of findings, and sharing those findings with the growing community of assessment scholars and practitioners (Banta and Associates, forthcoming). Some of the well-established lines of inquiry on which assessment scholarship can build include measurement, cognitive psychology, organizational development and change, and program evaluation.

While all of us wish it were otherwise, the scholarship of assessment in higher education is relatively rare. Mentkowski and Loacker and their colleagues at Alverno College have produced some of the most outstanding examples since they initiated the concept of assessment as learning in the early 1970s. As is evident in the articles in this issue by Erwin and DeMars and by Alexander L. Gabbin, systematic inquiry in assessment—particularly with regard to measurement issues—is currently under way at James Madison University (JMU). This began with Erwin's arrival at JMU in the early 1980s and is accelerating now that he and his colleagues in the Department of Psychology have inaugurated the nation's first doctoral program in outcomes assessment.

Additional sources of assessment scholarship are identified in this issue of *Assessment Update*. L. Roger Yin, Lance E. Urven, Robert M. Schramm, and Stephen J. Friedman are conducting studies of the impact of on-line learning at the University of Wisconsin-Whitewater. Mika Cho and Edward Forde at California State University, Los Angeles, are investigating students' learning styles in order to make informed recommendations to faculty about the use of diverse instructional strategies in their classes.

In *Building a Scholarship of Assessment*, we distinguish between the scholarship of assessment and *scholarly assessment*, the work being undertaken on hundreds of campuses to select or create assessment methods, try them out, reflect on their strengths and weaknesses, then modify the methods or try new ones in the spirit of continuously improving assessment practice. On the basis of what we have learned from roughly two decades of scholarly assessment, we have derived seventeen characteristics that distinguish effective practice (Banta and Associates, forthcoming). These characteristics can be clustered in three phases: (1) planning, (2) implementing, and (3) sustaining and improving the process.

Finally, we suggest some future directions for scholarship related to outcomes assessment. As much as we want to forge ahead in solving psychometric problems associated with our instruments and extending our knowledge of cognitive and psychosocial development, we must first address a formidable barrier to assessment: that of engaging a critical mass of faculty on each campus in cultural transformation that relies on data derived from assessment to provide direction for continuous improvement. In the book we suggest several strategies for thus engaging faculty. We also offer directions for future research in organizational behavior and development, measurement methodology, and the development of shared reflective practice. With respect to the last of these, a call is issued for a national effort to educate faculty about joint reflection on the results of assessment that can lead to collaborative action in making improvements suggested by the data.

After two decades of practice in assessing the outcomes of higher education, the field seems stuck in a rut. The same experiences are being repeated over and over in different settings because so few scholars are engaged in systematic study of the effects of various approaches. We need a well-grounded, vigorous scholarship of assessment to convince the skeptics who still believe outcomes assessment is a fad that in fact this is an interdisciplinary area with deep roots and developing stems that could support magnificent blossoms any day now! Dear reader, please contribute to this scholarship, and share it with us here in *Assessment Update*.

References

Banta, T. W. (2002). Preface. In T. W. Banta and Associates (Eds.), *Building a Scholarship of Assessment*. San Francisco, CA: Jossey-Bass.

Boyer, E. L. (1990). *Scholarship Reconsidered: Priorities for the Professoriate*. Princeton, NJ: Carnegie Foundation for the Advancement of Teaching.

How Do We Know Whether We Are Making a Difference?

Look for a variety of methods for making a difference using assessment described in interviews with eleven top administrators at institutions across the country. From Assessment Update 18:2 (2006).

What can we learn from the leaders of institutions noted for outstanding work in outcomes assessment? With a warrant from the editorial board of Assessment Update and support from a grant from the Tobias Center on Leadership at Indiana University-Purdue University Indianapolis, I recently explored this question in telephone interviews with eleven top administrators, including present or former chief executive officers (CEOs), chief academic officers (CAOs), or chief student affairs officers, at eleven institutions, from community colleges to research universities, located across the country. In a series of columns, I intend to share the perspectives of these leaders on a variety of topics. For a glimpse of the full range of their responses, please see the

April 2006 issue of Effective Practices for Academic Leaders *from Stylus Publishers.*

I asked my sample of senior administrators, "What assessment methods have proven most useful in providing direction for improvement on your campus?" What a wide variety of responses that produced!

Charles Schroeder, former vice president for student affairs at the University of Missouri-Columbia, said, "I had to break a very bad habit on the part of a lot of student affairs folk—the bad habit of saying to me, 'We did 300 programs in the residence halls,' implying that 'We're good because we did 300 things.'" Schroeder followed with his own questions: "How many people came to the programs? Did they like what you did? Did the programs make any difference? How do you know?"

Schroeder asked counseling center staff to dig into their data on individual counseling sessions to see if they could discern any patterns. The staff found that a very high percentage of women with bulimia were majors in a single academic unit. This information enabled Schroeder to suggest to the dean and faculty leaders in that unit that they might wish to explore whether students there were experiencing unusual kinds of pressure.

Instead of talking first about methods in his graduate course on assessment, Schroeder began by asking students, "How do we know if what we do makes a difference?" "That's assessment," Schroeder asserts.

Earl Lazerson, emeritus president at Southern Illinois University-Edwardsville (SIUE), wanted to make sure that much of what was done at SIUE was perceived in the community as making a difference. He valued "external validation—getting outside opinions in a more systematic way." He obtained faculty senate approval for a funded program of bringing community stakeholders in "to interact for a couple of days with our students and the respective faculty." Lazerson says, "I wouldn't call them external examiners, but it gets close to that. [That practice] started opening up the doors and windows a little."

External examiners, actually *external assessors*, as they are called, *are* used at Alverno College. Austin Doherty, emeritus CAO at Alverno, describes the process: "External assessors provide a wonderful experience for our students because [the students] receive feedback from professionals in the community who are not their teachers. It has been helpful for us to train our external assessors to be good critics. Then they can tell us what worked most effectively and how we might improve. They have become colleagues." One example of the use of external assessors involves a small business course in which students must write a business plan. Faculty members contact bankers in Milwaukee "who are willing to have students visit and present their plans, then provide critique—Is this a plan for which the bank would be willing to provide a loan?"

External assessment is also important to Michael Durrer, emeritus CAO at Mt. Hood Community College. As Durrer sees it, "There are three major components of assessment: self-evaluation by program faculty, external peer review, and assessment by customers such as students and employers. All three add greatly to the credibility of assessment in the eyes of the faculty, students, administrators, and the community. It is critical that the process maintain input from all the stakeholders."

Using data to demonstrate that a unit is making a difference can attract new resources at Samford University. CEO Tom Corts says, "We have tried to put money where there were good efforts and significant differences being made. Our education school, our pharmacy school, those are two units that have led in this, and we've put additional money into both . . . when we have had new funds to allocate."

Assessing prior learning in writing, math, critical thinking, and use of technology with instruments created by faculty is making a difference at James Madison University (JMU), reports provost Douglas Brown. "We feed the information from pretesting back to the high schools where we see difficulty or where we see that they are doing a superb job. . . . SAT scores and transcripts are such poor predictors that our assessment instruments turn out to be the best predictors of what a student will do." Assessment of JMU sophomores "demonstrates that our students are or are not meeting the standards we've set. That's incredibly valuable on a couple of levels—first in terms of feedback to the students. But it's equally valuable in providing feedback to instructors on their teaching methods, specifically, how we can improve methods in areas like mathematics and writing. As a consequence, the pedagogy in intermediate and advanced mathematics has improved dramatically."

While faculty at JMU have chosen to develop their own assessment instruments, nationally standardized instruments have helped to make a difference at the University of Charleston. As former provost Margaret Malmberg puts it, "The data that we take from students on the Academic Profile, the California Test of Critical Thinking, and the National Survey of Student Engagement, we give back to the students. That is, we tell them individually how they do. This requires that faculty take the instruments . . . so that they know what they're about. Talking with students about how they did will help them know how they stand and what they might need to do to make improvements in their performance."

Electronic student portfolios enable faculty and students to see whether instruction is making a difference at Alverno College and at the University of Charleston. The individual student is the chief beneficiary of the use of electronic portfolios at Alverno. As Austin Doherty describes it, "We now have a *diagnostic* digital portfolio—not a portfolio of [students'] best work. [The portfolio] is based on our curriculum so that students can put in . . . some key performances, faculty feedback, and the student's self-assessment. When students give speeches, these are videotaped—that's the only way the student can see herself and make a judgment about her performance. . . . The student will use [the videotape] to see her performance over a period of time and make judgments about what has been improving and what she still needs to improve. It's diagnostic rather than just putting in a few great performances. She and the faculty use [the portfolio] as another learning tool as well as an assessment instrument."

Group assessment is the focus of portfolios at the University of Charleston. According to Malmberg, "We want to capture not just individual student work but also [group work as] a way to look at critical thinking across students and across years." Malmberg has discovered what many others experimenting with electronic portfolios have learned: it is a time-consuming process. She says, a bit ruefully, "When you have a complex agenda, it makes it more difficult. My systematic approach is very ambitious. I didn't just want something that would allow students to put their work somewhere. I was absolutely sure that we needed a way to analyze change in student behavior over time. That requires a more sophisticated storage and integration system."

Finally, involving faculty in the scholarship of assessment is the way academic leaders are trying to make a difference with assessment at the U.S. Naval Academy and the Georgia Institute of Technology. William Miller, provost at the U.S. Naval Academy, told me, "We try to use standardized instruments where they appear to be measuring what we're interested in and where you get good results. But in some cases, we have to become part of the research side of assessment and develop approaches. Our mission starts out to develop midshipmen morally, mentally, and physically. Physically is easy. Mentally is at least approachable. But talking about how one develops a person's character—their moral development—is really tough. We find that we're now out there on the leading edge nationally, working with the Canadian armed forces to develop some approaches to measuring character development."

Jack Lohmann, vice provost at Georgia Tech, finds that the engineering faculty who predominate there find surveys helpful. He says, "Despite skepticism about the benefit-cost ratio, when faculty get the [survey] data, by and large they will respond to it. They will take it to heart and think about what it means in terms of the quality of their educational programs." But Lohmann worries most about direct measures of learning outcomes—what students can actually do. "It requires a fair amount of serious scholarly research to do that well," he says, and he has found this "a pretty tough thing to push" with colleagues. A boost for Lohmann in this regard has been a quality enhancement plan required of Georgia Tech for reaccreditation by the Southern Association of Colleges and Schools. Georgia Tech's plan is designed to enhance global competence, and success will be demonstrated, in part, by assessing students' global competence. Lohmann's strategy is to "break assessment down into projects or activities in which faculty are already engaged, like the quality enhancement plan. Then I can demonstrate proof of concept, that one can do this stuff and do it meaningfully. By the way, you can even get resources [grant funds] to do it. You can write papers and publish, you contribute to the body of knowledge, and in the process you will actually help to improve the educational environment. That's the direction we're trying to move in."

Obviously, there is no single best measure of making a difference with assessment. Institutional and disciplinary characteristics help to determine which measures will provide credible evidence in a given environment. Faculty at Alverno appreciate the contributions of external examiners to their assessment efforts, and at SIUE, visits by community stakeholders "opened the doors and windows a little." While faculty at the University of Charleston prefer nationally standardized tests, those at James Madison University are most satisfied with instruments they have developed themselves. The single cross-cutting theme is that the best question to ask as assessment gets under way is, "What evidence do we need to convince ourselves that we are making a difference in student learning?"

Demonstrating the Impact of Changes Based on Assessment Findings

Look for some reasons for the paucity of evidence that assessment is improving student learning over time. From Assessment Update 21:2 (2009).

In the November–December issue of *Assessment Update* (Volume 20, Number 6), I introduced a forthcoming book that now has the title *Designing Effective Assessment: Principles and Profiles of Good Practice* (Jossey-Bass, in press). My coauthors Elizabeth Jones and Karen Black and I invited more than 1,000 individuals to contribute profiles of good practice for this volume. We received 146 profiles and used 49 of these in full in our text to illustrate principles of good practice in planning, implementing, and improving or sustaining assessment. Now we are developing a series of articles for *Assessment Update* that are based on aggregated information derived from the profiles.

Each profile was prepared in a common format, using an outline that we provided. In addition to a full description of the assessment approach, we asked about the findings that the approach generated, the uses made of those findings, and the impact of using the findings. Here I will present what we learned about impact.

In asking about the impact of using findings in our outline for profile authors, we hoped to learn about the long-term effects of implementing assessment. Most important, had student learning improved? Could the profile authors cite evidence that improving instruction or some aspect of student support services had made a difference in academic achievement, student retention, or satisfaction of students or graduates?

Just 9 of the 146 profiles we collected (6 percent) contained evidence that student learning had improved over time. For example, Teresa Flateby and her colleagues at the University of South Florida have data showing that student writing has improved as a result of using their rubric, the Cognitive Level and Quality of Writing Assessment (CLAQWA). The rubric incorporates five major categories, each with multiple traits, and five operationally defined performance levels. Use of the CLAQWA enables faculty to construct assignments that develop progressively more complex levels of learning.

At North Carolina State University, Patti Clayton and her colleagues have demonstrated improvements in students' reasoning and critical thinking skills in connection with outcomes such as civic learning and personal growth. They use a reflection model called DEAL, an acronym derived from the steps of description, examination, and articulation of learning. DEAL provides prompts to guide critical thinking and a rubric for scoring students' reflection products.

At San José State University, use of faculty-developed rubrics over time shows that providing more writing practice earlier in the student experience has enabled all graduating students to exhibit at least minimal levels of writing and speaking skills. Similarly, use of a locally developed tool provides evidence that students at James Madison University have mastered required skills in information literacy. At two other universities, faculty who have used rubrics in their own classes report that students' writing and analytic skills, respectively, have improved as a result.

I am pleased that Mark Lencho, Michael Longrie, and Stephen Friedman have given us another example of improvement in learning in this issue of *Assessment Update*. Using a rubric developed by writing faculty at the University of Wisconsin-Whitewater, the authors and their colleagues were able to document improvements over time in students' attainment of three general education goals.

The overwhelming majority (137) of the profiles we received summarized the impact of using assessment findings in terms of improved academic processes rather than outcomes. In order of frequency of mention, the following improvements were cited:

- Increased campus awareness of the need to identify learning outcomes and assess student achievement of them, resulting in more assessment activity

- More work designed to strengthen assessment tools such as exams and rubrics

- More professional development activities offered and utilized, enabling faculty and staff to teach and assess more effectively

- More use of assessment findings

- Redesign of programs, courses, and assignments to address assessed learner weaknesses

- Accreditation requirements met and, in some cases, direction obtained for campuswide quality improvement efforts

- Approval and funding for new positions—faculty to address learning weaknesses and staff to enhance assessment capabilities

Given that the history of assessing institutional outcomes (particularly student learning) now spans more than two decades, we were disappointed to find so little tangible evidence of improved outcomes in the profiles collected for our book. While the lengthy list of institutional processes that have been improved on the basis of guidance obtained from assessment findings is impressive, it is outcomes that our stakeholders now insist that we measure and report. A few possible explanations for the lack of focus on improved outcomes occurred to us.

First, our inquiry about the length of time that the profiled assessment initiative had been in place revealed that 90, or 62 percent, had a history of fewer than five years. It often takes at least two years to collect sufficient data to convince faculty that a change is needed. Then it may take another year or two to craft and implement an appropriate change and another two years to collect data on the impact of the change. Perhaps our sample of profiles simply contained too many immature examples.

On the other hand, we may have obtained a representative sample of assessment approaches; few projects of any kind in the academy are planned, implemented, and monitored for five years or more. Priorities and personnel change, and interest in follow-up wanes.

So far, the emphasis within most colleges and universities has been on specifying outcomes and developing mechanisms for assessing the outcomes, then taking warranted actions based on the assessment findings. Few have talked about following up to see whether the changes undertaken have produced the desired improvements or whether improvements can be sustained over time. Again, faculty move on to other priorities, the characteristics of the students involved change, or additional program modifications undertaken for other reasons make it difficult to gauge only the impact of the original changes made in response to assessment findings.

Finally, perhaps it is the case that too few of our colleagues appreciate the role they might play in providing evidence to parents of students and to trustees, governors, and legislators of the effectiveness of the educational programs for which they are responsible. To date, our favorite assessment tools have been exams, rubrics, and questionnaires we have designed ourselves. Can we aggregate data from these homemade instruments and report the information in ways that satisfy our stakeholders? Then, can we make changes that the data tell us are desirable and continue to monitor and report outcomes in ways that demonstrate continuous improvement to our stakeholders? If we cannot, our stakeholders will inevitably insist that standardized tests become our primary assessment tools for the foreseeable future. While these tests are expensive and measure only a small portion of the learning outcomes we consider important, many of those who provide funding for higher education believe that they can provide a stable monitoring system for tracking the impact of using assessment findings over time.

One Bird's-Eye View of the U.S. Landscape for Assessment

Take Part in the National Goals Debate

Look for some of the measurement concerns to be addressed as the National Center for Education Statistics considers developing a national test for college students. From Assessment Update 4:1 *(1992).*

President Bush, Secretary of Education Lamar Alexander, and the nation's governors have agreed on six national goals for education that provide the basis for the America 2000 program of educational improvement. While this program is aimed principally at the K–12 sector, the involvement of higher education is essential in preparing teachers, upgrading workforce skills, and shedding light on the best methods of promoting and assessing student development. In addition, National Goal 5, Objective 5, touches directly the interests of those of us concerned about assessment in higher education. That objective is stated, "[By the year 2000] the proportion of college graduates who demonstrate an advanced ability to think critically, communicate effectively, and solve problems will increase substantially."

The first annual progress report on the achievement of the national goals, which was issued on September 30, 1991, did not include any information on achievement of Objective 5.5. However, its section "Indicators for Future Reports" contained an expression of hope that indicators could be developed for the abilities of college students to think critically, communicate effectively, and solve problems.

Members of the National Education Goals Panel and others involved in guiding implementation of the America 2000 strategies are advocating the use of multiple measures in any national assessment system that may be developed; that is, multiple-choice tests would be supplemented with performance-based or portfolio assessments. But the American Psychological Association, the American Educational Research Association, and the National Council on Measurement in Education have issued a joint statement urging caution in moving to base a national system on these relatively new and unproven technologies without considerable exploration of the complex technical issues involved.

As Donald Stewart points out in the lead article in this issue, experienced assessment practitioners know that we must also be concerned about achieving consensus on the goals of assessment and on the learning outcomes to be measured. What effects will the very process of trying to reach this consensus in higher education have on the scope of college curricula, on academic freedom, on institutional diversity?

We also know that students must be motivated to do their best work if assessment is to be valid. What consequences will be associated with student performance on a national examination system? The response to this question may have the effect of limiting the opportunity to obtain a college degree and ultimately restricting access to higher education.

Finally, we are painfully aware that assessment in and of itself does not produce educational improvements. Assessment must be linked to specific outcome-oriented objectives, which are systematically implemented with appropriate human and technical resources. Only if these connections are explicit can assessment findings be used effectively to suggest directions for improvement.

A decade of widespread experience in assessing the outcomes of higher education has produced a number of important principles, which should be considered in the debate surrounding design and implementation of a national assessment system, especially one that includes a postsecondary component. We have learned that faculty, students, and other stakeholders must be involved in setting the goals and objectives for learning and assessment; that these objectives must be used in the classroom to shape teaching and student development; that students must accept responsibility for their own learning and performance on assessment measures; that we must employ a variety of assessment techniques; and perhaps most importantly, that we must build assessment into ongoing processes that matter to faculty, so that they will use assessment findings to improve curricula and methods of instruction. Now is the time to share what we have learned with decision makers who hope to improve education in this country.

Find out what the governor of your state is doing to promote the America 2000 goals, and volunteer to serve on task forces and advisory groups—even if the current focus of their activity is K–12 education. You can contribute to early discussions about reforms at that level, thus establishing credibility as a resource when the debate turns to assessment in higher education.

Sal Corallo reported in the November–December 1991 issue of *Assessment Update* that the National Center for Education Statistics (NCES) has asked 15 individuals with a diverse array of scholarly interests, from the definition of critical thinking to the evaluation of new response modes for standardized tests, to contribute position papers on the implementation of Objective 5.5. The operative word here is implementation—the writers were instructed to raise questions and concerns if they wished but to give NCES the benefit of their best thinking about how the objective should be operationalized, because it *will* be implemented in one way or another.

The NCES panel of 15 includes 5 people with particular interest in higher education assessment: Georgine Loacker and Marcia Mentkowski of Alverno College, Peter Ewell of the National Center for Higher Education Management Systems, James Ratcliff from Penn State, and myself. Any and all of us would be pleased to hear how you are becoming involved in the conversation about the national goals. I would be delighted to publish your letters on this topic or to quote from them in this space.

Do Faculty Sense the Tightening of the Accountability Noose?

Look for a summary of activities surrounding plans to develop a national test for postsecondary students focused on the skills of communicating, problem solving, and critical thinking. From Assessment Update 5:4 (1993).

Academic year 1992–93 was sobering for those of us who hope that conscientious implementation of outcomes assessment can be a significant factor in enabling colleges and universities to demonstrate their worth to external constituencies. Ever-increasing competition between higher education and a diverse array of social services for ever-scarcer public funds and among a diverse array of providers for commitment from those shopping for educational services has led to more intense external scrutiny of our institutions than ever before.

To provide a sampling of the forms this scrutiny has taken: the public perception that research activities are diverting faculty time and attention from undergraduate teaching has led legislatures and governing boards to undertake inquiries into how faculty are spending their time. Regional and disciplinary associations have become more diligent in seeking evidence that institutions are seriously engaged in assessing outcomes. A task force appointed by the National Governors' Association (NGA) has recommended implementing a national performance-based assessment for a sample of postsecondary students to measure progress toward the national goal (National Goal 5, Objective 5, to be precise) of increasing "the proportion of college graduates who demonstrate an advanced ability to think critically, communicate effectively, and solve problems." And the National Center on Education Statistics (NCES) has issued a request for proposals to initiate the first phase of this national assessment.

I have found myself right in the middle of all of this. Within three months of my arrival, my new institution was reviewed by the North Central Association and was subsequently instructed to develop by January

1995 a formal plan for assessing student learning. The trustees of Indiana University asked us for a report on the nature of faculty work and the means being used to evaluate it. The NGA invited me to join Peter Ewell and measurement expert Stephen Dunbar from the University of Iowa in a public debate with the chair of its task force on postsecondary assessment. Despite my strong reservations about the development of a national test, I agreed to contribute ideas to a consortium of organizations submitting a proposal to NCES for the first phase of this development.

We have ample evidence, especially from the experience of elementary and secondary schools over the last quarter-century, that testing alone does not improve learning. In fact, far from having produced exemplary levels of learning, achievement testing in grades K–12 now reveals some serious deficits in fundamental skills for U.S. students as compared with their age peers in many other countries. These findings are among the most influential reasons for the growing interest in restructuring local schools and school systems.

The development of performance-based assessment for a sample of postsecondary students will be enormously expensive and will not in and of itself improve the learning of college students. Realization of Goal 5, Objective 5 requires that (1) the skills of communicating, problem solving, and critical thinking at a level acceptable for college graduates can be operationally defined, (2) a substantial proportion of U.S. faculty will agree with the definitions and teach the skills in ways that are effective in promoting student learning of them, (3) valid measures of the defined skills can be devised, (4) a truly representative sample of students can be induced to participate in the national assessment and to take this exercise seriously and perform conscientiously, and (5) the assessment results will be used to improve teaching and other aspects of the educational experience for undergraduates.

Once again drawing on the experience of our K–12 colleagues, we know that this sequence of activities can best be carried out at the local level in individual colleges and universities and in individual classrooms. Why do we have to spend years of precious time and millions of dollars of public funds to find this out?

Perhaps a large expenditure of time and money is necessary if only to call faculty and administrators' attention to the public's concern about the outcomes of higher education.

The NGA has sponsored a series of hearings on the issue of national postsecondary assessment. Despite the fact that they have been scheduled in conjunction with the annual meetings of several large national organizations that have a substantial number of members from academia, the hearings have not drawn large audiences. For example, the testimony heard by NGA in Atlanta in one of the hotels hosting the American Educational Research Association (AERA) conference, which annually attracts six to eight thousand people, drew no more than 20 AERA members for the NGA audience.

The accountability noose is being drawn ever more tightly, and ultimately this fact will become clear to faculty throughout academe. As more voices are heard in opposition to the national postsecondary assessment plan and the actual costs of the enterprise become known to those who must fund it, this particular train may well be derailed. But in the meantime, the NCES is making sure that the train leaves the station on the first leg of its journey—the objective-setting phase—and I hope some of us who have the benefit of campus-based experience in outcomes assessment are at least on board ready to give advice to the engineer about the curves and obstacles ahead.

Can We Combine Peer Review and National Assessment?

Look for developments at a December 1995 meeting convened to consider how the National Center for Education Statistics might assist states in assessing student learning of the skills of communicating, problem solving, and critical thinking. From Assessment Update 8:2 (1996).

In early December 1995 I took part in a meeting in Washington that might be considered the end of an era. Or was it the beginning of another? We won't know the answer until the full impact of congressional intentions to make block grants to the states is apparent.

Sal Corrallo, senior staff member at the National Center for Education Statistics (NCES), and project director of the National Assessment of College Student Learning, called the meeting. *Assessment Update* readers will recall that Corrallo has led the effort to identify ways to measure college graduates' abilities to think critically, solve problems, and communicate effectively, the skills associated with National Education Goal 5.5, now 6.5 (see Corrallo's article in *Assessment Update*, Vol. 6, No. 3, pp. 5, 7, 11). Corrallo plans to retire in March 1996, and the result of the conference in Washington was to close the door on the federal effort he has shepherded and to test the feasibility of opening a door on future state efforts in this area.

The December conference was designed to acknowledge what NCES has been able to accomplish to date in connection with Goal 6.5 and to answer the question, Can NCES help states assess the student learning described in Goal 6.5? Those invited to attend the conference and join in this conversation were higher education executive officers in the 50 states, their representatives, or both, as well as a sprinkling of those of us with long-time interests in implementing postsecondary assessment. Joe M. Steele, one of the conference presenters, has prepared a summary of his remarks as the lead article in this issue.

The NCES role has been quiet, but significant. In 1991, 15 of us were commissioned to write papers describing some of the issues surrounding national assessment of college student learning. Our papers were reviewed by an additional 30 individuals, and the 45 of us gathered in Washington in November 1991 for an initial discussion. A similar sequence of activities took place in 1992 in connection with a second set of commissioned papers. Following the second meeting, the National Center for Postsecondary Teaching, Learning, and Assessment at Penn State received NCES funding to conduct a series of Delphi studies designed to characterize the learning outcomes associated with the

Goal 6.5 abilities of thinking critically, communicating, and solving problems. In addition, Peter Ewell and Dennis Jones of NCHEMS were commissioned to identify indicators of good practice that might constitute indirect measures of the three abilities. Both of these research projects provided evidence that it is possible to achieve agreement among postsecondary educators concerning the definitions of the complex skills sought by the National Education Goals Panel.

Hoping to build on the several activities initiated in 1991, Corrallo and others at NCES issued a request for proposals (RFP) in 1993 that, had the federal funding come through, would have produced a framework for assessing levels of achievement in each of the three Goal 6.5 areas as well as examples of assessment approaches. For 1996, NCES had planned to issue another RFP for the deployment of a national assessment of college student learning in the three areas. But in the aftermath of the 1994 congressional elections, the future of all National Education Goals activities is very much in question.

The December 1995 meeting produced a number of suggestions in connection with the basic question. In order to strengthen state assessment efforts, if that is to be the level at which the principal action will occur in higher education policy-making, NCES was encouraged to promote the development of state and regional networks of people interested in assessment by means of newsletters, listservs, World Wide Web sites, and state-supported pilot projects.

As I listened to the dialogue, another approach occurred to me. Sal Corrallo had asked me to report on Tennessee's experience with performance funding. As I have reported previously in this column, a study I conducted recently with Linda Rudolph, Janice Van Dyke, and Homer Fisher (*Assessment Update*, Vol. 6, No. 4, pp. 3, 14) suggested that peer review is the performance funding activity most productive of improvement on campuses in Tennessee. This includes program reviews conducted by individual campuses as well as disciplinary accreditation reviews. Over the years I have noted that most programs that are subject to disciplinary accreditation pay more attention to the need for assessment than those that are not guided by an accreditation body. Similarly, institutions tend to become most active in carrying out assessment just prior to the time of their ten-year regional reaccreditation process when that process emphasizes outcomes. I began to wonder if the answer to the NCES question about perpetuating its assessment emphasis might be to strengthen the assessment mechanisms utilized by disciplinary and regional accreditation bodies.

Federal influence on accreditation organizations in the realm of outcomes assessment is not new. In 1988 Secretary of Education William Bennett issued an executive order requiring these bodies to include assessment criteria in their guidelines if they were interested in recognition from his office. But despite the fact that most accreditors now have such criteria, not all have found effective ways to define and enforce them.

The public's interest in holding colleges and universities accountable for increasing student learning of critically needed citizenship and workplace skills is strong and growing stronger. Institutions must find ways of providing credible evidence of student learning that are acceptable to educators as well as to the public. Few in academe relish the thought of having either federal or state government officials tell them how student achievement will be assessed. The judgment of respected peers is the evaluation mechanism of choice for most academics. Thus, one sensible approach is to make the assessment of student outcomes as well as program and institutional effectiveness a central part of the peer review associated with disciplinary and regional accreditation. In this way we can accommodate the federal (and state) interest in assessing learning within the framework of peer judgment that is most acceptable to faculty and administrators.

Although the national coordinating body known as the Council on Postsecondary Accreditation was disbanded in 1993, national leaders in higher education are working now to win institutional approval of plans for a new such organization, which would be called the Council for Higher Education Accreditation (CHEA). Leadership for CHEA would be provided by a board of directors composed of current chief executive officers of colleges and universities and trustees who are widely representative of the professions and the public at large.

For years colleges and universities have been providing information to NCES via surveys that form the foundation of the Integrated Postsecondary Education Data System (IPEDS). IPEDS surveys, which are completed by all providers of postsecondary education, currently are focused primarily on the collection of input data: student enrollments, faculty salaries, and institutional finances. But couldn't CHEA draw on its member institutions for the faculty experts needed to work with IPEDS in developing appropriate national indicators of student learning and institutional effectiveness? If so, NCES could utilize the national system that supports the peer review that academics value to collect the kinds of data about student and institutional outcomes that governments and the public find credible.

Trying to Clothe the Emperor

Look for a description of some of the issues that must be confronted as policy-makers worldwide seek a quick way to determine what students learn in college so that institutions can be compared. From Assessment Update 20:2 *(2008).*

Since last I wrote to you about accountability testing, the train has left the station and is picking up steam. The very large California State University and University of Texas systems are administering the Collegiate Learning Assessment on every campus. In December 2007, the presidents of the member institutions of the National Association of State Universities and Land-Grant Colleges voted to make the Voluntary System of Accountability (VSA) available to all members who wish to use it (http://www.voluntarysystem.org/index.cfm) . The VSA is a reporting system that uses a few standard measures to characterize postsecondary institutions and thus make some comparisons possible. The VSA includes as one of its non-negotiable components a form of value-added measurement based on scores derived from one of the following standardized tests of generic skills: the Collegiate Assessment of Academic Proficiency (CAAP) from ACT, the Measure of Academic Proficiency and Progress (MAPP) from Educational Testing Service (ETS), and the Collegiate Learning Assessment (CLA) from the Council for Aid to Education (CAE). In addition, in November, the Paris-based international Organisation for Economic Co-operation and Development convened a meeting in Korea in which representatives of Korea, Japan, the European Union, the United States, and several other member countries decided to pursue a pilot project aimed at developing a test of culturally relevant tasks that will purport to measure college students' critical thinking abilities in countries around the world. It seems that policymakers everywhere are interested in finding a quick way to determine what students are learning in college, so that they can compare institutions.

It doesn't seem to matter that the measurement instruments currently available and being considered for this easy fix are not up to the task in terms of logic or psychometrics. While CAAP and MAPP have been used appropriately to provide feedback about knowledge and skills to individual students and to suggest to faculty areas in which additional work is needed to strengthen generic skills for groups of students, the new use of these tests and the CLA to assess and compare the quality of institutions cannot be supported with data collected to date. In this column and elsewhere in *Assessment Update* (see Volume 18, Number 4; Volume 19, Number 1; and Volume 19, Number 6), we have tried to brief you on some of the problems. Let me recap this literature briefly, without references, and ask that you consult the originals if you are interested.

1. The tests being recommended—standardized tests of writing, critical thinking, and analytic reasoning—are first and foremost tests of prior learning, as evidenced by the near-perfect .9 correlation between CLA scores and SAT/ACT scores at the institutional level.

2. This high correlation between scores on the recommended tests and the level of skills and abilities students bring with

them when they enter college means that some 80 percent of the variance in scores between and among institutions is accounted for by prior learning. From the remaining 20 percent, we must subtract the important effects of differences in institutions' student populations (for example, differences in age, gender, race or ethnicity, and socioeconomic status). Some of the remaining variance is undoubtedly due to other confounding factors such as motivation to do well on the test, test anxiety, sampling error, error of measurement, and college major. In calculating growth (score gain) from freshman to senior years, student maturation is another critical factor that must be accounted for before we can consider the component of the variation that may be due to the impact of a particular institution on student learning. Do we want our institutions to be judged on an impact that accounts, at best, for 1–2 percent of the variance in institutional scores on these tests?

3. The evidence of the technical quality of the recommended tests that has been provided by the test publishers is woefully inadequate. Current data on test-retest reliability are not available; construct and content validity studies are sparse to nonexistent, depending on the instrument being considered; current norms are based only on the small samples of institutions that have seen fit to use these tests to date; longitudinal studies designed to tell whether students attending college for six years do better on the tests than individuals of similar ability who have not spent the same six years in college have not been conducted. Gary Pike identifies additional threats to validity in his Assessment Measures column in this issue.

4. In an effort to remove prior learning as a source of variation, the application of regression analyses is being proposed so that institutions' raw test scores are not the

measure being reported and thus compared. Instead, the very controversial measure referred to as *value added*—freshman-to-senior score gain, if any—will be used. A review of the literature reveals that value-added statistics can differ significantly, depending on the method of calculation used; and the reliability of all the value-added measures is about .1, just slightly better than chance.

5. No set of tasks or items designed to test generic skills like writing and reasoning is content-free. Students in engineering, art, and anthropology are being taught to write and reason like scholars in these disciplines, and each discipline has its unique ways of collecting and communicating information. When students in these fields are confronted with the test stimuli in CAAP, MAPP, or CLA, they will react differently; some will be advantaged by their choice of major, and others will be disadvantaged.

6. And speaking of *students* (who are almost being ignored in the current conversation about accountability!), all the research on motivation is being tossed aside, if considered at all, by those behind the press to assess with a test. In order to avoid outrageous costs, institutions are being encouraged to think that they can entice *samples* of students to take these tests. Extrinsic sources of motivation such as cash payments and chances to win a lottery may work in luring a student in, but these offers will not guarantee that once on site a student will do his or her best work or even finish the test, nor will they ensure that a first-year student will return to take the test as a senior to make possible the crucial value-added calculation.

7. Since sampling will not, in all probability, yield the number of intrinsically motivated students needed over time to carry out valid accountability testing, institutions will see the need to make participation in assessment mandatory for all

students. This takes considered faculty action and time to institute and enforce, as institutions in Tennessee, Missouri, and elsewhere discovered in the 1980s when the first wave of accountability testing was launched. Not every student must be tested, but every student must participate in some form of assessment if equal protection is to be achieved. And we will need to find ways to provide *intrinsic* motivation for *all* students so that they will perform conscientiously on the instruments selected for their campus.

8. No matter what we are being told now about the reasons for administering these tests, without question, institutions' "scores," however they come to be defined, will be compared—as if they have real meaning and reflect truth. Then what? Will some institutions be castigated publicly because their students are (supposedly) failing to gain as much in college as students at some other institutions? Will students ultimately be discouraged from attending these institutions? Will funding for these institutions be withheld or corrective actions imposed by state or federal governments, as is the case in the K–12 sector? Will institutions develop prep courses to help students improve their scores on these tests? Will private consultants and companies profit from coaching students in order to improve their scores?

Dear colleagues, *the emperor has no clothes*. While appropriate for giving individual students and faculty ideas about strengths and weaknesses and areas of curriculum and instruction to improve, the standardized tests of generic skills being touted today are just not capable of fulfilling the dreams of policymakers who want to assess and *compare* the capacities of institutions (and nations) to improve college student learning.

Yet we seem headed irreversibly for a future in which accountability testing will have a prominent role. Millions of hours of faculty, staff, and student time and millions of dollars will be spent on this endeavor, and it will be years before the steam powering this locomotive peters out.

So, is there any way to put clothes on this emperor? There certainly are some things that we can and should do if our leaders volunteer our campuses for testing. And there is no shortage of good experience to guide us, since hundreds of institutions across the country have used standardized tests like CAAP and the College Basic Academic Subjects Exam (developed at the University of Missouri) over the last twenty years to supplement their understanding of learning through assessment.

When I was serving on the Learning Outcomes Working Group associated with the VSA, I was unsuccessful in turning the tide against including standardized tests of generic skills in the institutional reporting template that ultimately emerged. I was able, however, to encourage the VSA developers to include in the instructions accompanying the template some advice for the test purveyors and some suggestions for faculty and staff considering use of the tests. In the first instance, we asked ACT, ETS, and CAE to beef up the evidence they provide of the reliability and validity of their instruments. In September, I was encouraged to see that a $2.4 million grant from the Fund for the Improvement of Postsecondary Education (FIPSE) would provide support for some of that work. My spirits fell, however, when I learned that the principal investigator for the test validation portion of the FIPSE project would be one of the most prominent spokespersons for the CLA. I fear that the FIPSE-supported findings related to CAAP, MAPP, and CLA will suffer the same fate as studies of drug efficacy sponsored by pharmaceutical companies, considered suspect due to the obvious source of investigator bias.

So clothing the emperor is up to those of us on individual campuses who care about using assessment to provide direction for improving learning. In the instructions accompanying the VSA, we offered some of the following suggestions for institutions that decide to use one of the three tests:

1. Involve respected faculty and staff *and* student leaders in studying the three recommended tests. If faculty and staff are not involved in selecting the test to be used, they will not be

likely to find the scores useful in any way. And if the results of testing are not used to improve anything, what good are they? In addition, if faculty are not convinced of the meaning and usefulness of the test scores, their hearts and minds will not be engaged in developing forms of intrinsic motivation for students to take the tests and perform conscientiously.

2. Ask faculty and students to compare the names and descriptions of the scales that make up each test to the stated goals and objectives for general education at your institution. To what extent is there a match in the content and intent of the scales? Research suggests that none of the tests will assess more than 25 percent of the goals considered important, but finding even a few matches may be helpful in establishing the most basic type of validity (face validity) for a given test and, thus, some confidence in it.

3. Give faculty and students on the selection committee an opportunity to take and review their scores on the test they perceive to be the best match with their goals. Asking that they predict their highest and lowest scores in advance may increase their interest in their scores as well as their motivation to give the test their best effort. And if the test maker is not willing to provide the full test or at least a comprehensive sample of items for this purpose, move on to another test. We know that faculty are not willing to buy a pig in a poke. In the 1980s, a national professional organization spent millions of grant dollars to develop a comprehensive test in its discipline. But faculty were not permitted to see the whole test before administering it. Since few were willing to purchase the test sight unseen, it was not used by many schools. Ultimately, it met an ignominious end; in a sort of fire sale, institutions were encouraged to purchase the item bank for their own use at a very nominal price, and the organization's capacity to offer comparative data was lost.

4. Ask a few students to take the test alone with a faculty observer, describing their thought processes aloud to the faculty member as they encounter each item. This is a time-consuming process, but it is the very best way to tell how students are experiencing each item, what information they bring to bear in responding, and, thus, in what areas alternative teaching strategies or curricular opportunities might be helpful in increasing students' understanding and performance.

5. Publicize the work of the faculty, staff, and students on the selection committee and involve faculty members in advocating that attention be paid to the results of testing because they have implications for improvements in teaching and curricula that can help the institution achieve its student learning goals in general education. Ask student members of the committee to work with other student leaders to encourage conscientious performance on the selected test because the institution's reputation is at stake and because the scores will be used to make improvements in learning opportunities.

6. Conduct your own studies that demonstrate the usefulness of the given test *on your campus*. If you don't have measurement experts among your faculty or staff, consider creating a consortium of institutions, with a leader who can design studies on a group of campuses to answer questions such as the following: How closely do the measures on the test match valued institutional goals? How motivated are students to do their best work? What incentives are effective in encouraging students to do their best work on the test? What demographic, motivational, or disciplinary major characteristics predict test scores best? How reliable and valid are scores? Is there a ceiling effect? (That is, do some students achieve such high scores as freshmen that they can't increase

their scores significantly as seniors and may, due to chance, even earn lower scores as seniors?) How reliable is the value-added measure? How can faculty actually *use* the test scores to improve learning?

As I have revealed in previous essays, I believe that standardized tests in major fields hold more promise than standardized tests of generic skills for providing data for any comparisons of institutional effectiveness that must be made. And ultimately, I feel sure that student electronic portfolios will give us the best evidence of growth in student learning over time. I am encouraged by the fact that a portion of the FIPSE grant mentioned earlier will examine the potential of e-portfolios for this purpose. But if we must try to clothe the emperor who stands before us today, the steps I have suggested may provide some assistance.

Are There Measures for Improvement and Accountability?

Look for a set of concerns related to using assessment to guide campus improvements versus using assessment to demonstrate accountability, when the definition of accountability is value added to student learning as measured by scores on a standardized test of generic skills. From Assessment Update 22:1 (2010).

For most of my career, I have been advising faculty and student development professionals on my own campus and elsewhere to select or design outcomes assessment measures that can both suggest direction for improvement and demonstrate accountability. In fact, I have gone so far as to assert that we risk wasting the time of faculty, students, and staff—not to mention the money spent on purchasing measuring instruments—if we adopt approaches to assessment that are intended only to satisfy the demands of external policymakers.

As I have offered this advice, I have had in mind the kind of accountability that most regional and disciplinary accreditors have been advocating over the last decade or so—that is, defining appropriate learning outcomes for our students, assessing student attainment of those outcomes, and using what we learn by looking at the performance of groups of students to make warranted changes in curriculum, pedagogy, and academic support programs.

But in 2006, the report of the Commission on the Future of Higher Education (U. S. Department of Education, 2006) changed the interpretation of the term *accountability*. In that report, colleges and universities are challenged to provide *accountability* data that will measure the value they add to student learning and that will permit comparisons among institutions on this element of performance. In the most visible response to the commission's report—the Voluntary System of Accountability (http://www.voluntarysystem.org/index.cfm)—it was assumed that standardized tests of generic skills would yield the most credible evidence of value added that could be compared across institutions.

Now I am beginning to wonder whether my advice about using the same measures to guide improvement and to demonstrate institutional accountability is still sound. Are there really measures that will do both, according to this new definition of *accountability?*

At the 2009 Assessment Institute in Indianapolis in October, I decided to take an informal poll related to this issue. I asked those among the 900 or so in the first plenary session who were using standardized tests of generic skills to stand. About 200 people rose. I asked that they remain standing if they believed that information gleaned from these standardized tests could be used to improve student learning. With an audible *whoosh!* as the air went out of the room, all but a handful of those who had been standing sat down. A majority returned to their feet when I asked whether they believed the tests could supply information for accountability purposes.

Then I repeated this sequence of questions for electronic portfolios, recognizing that this technology is growing in importance as faculty search for assessment alternatives that have credibility on campus. When I asked,

"Who is using e-portfolios?" perhaps 300 people rose. I asked those who believed that the information yielded by portfolios could be used to improve student learning to remain standing. Almost no one sat down. Then I asked those who believed that e-portfolios could yield information to demonstrate accountability to remain standing. Again, very few sat down.

Clearly, many of the individuals who attended the Assessment Institute believe that e-portfolios can serve the two purposes of guiding improvement and demonstrating accountability. I sincerely hope they are right. We certainly know that portfolios have credibility among faculty, students, and staff because they permit students to demonstrate their learning in a wide variety of ways, represent so much more than a time-bound snapshot of a small portion of a student's abilities, and provide a repository for showing gains in learning over time.

But can we develop rubrics that are reliable and valid in order to evaluate students' work in portfolios? Teresa Flateby at the University of South Florida and Marilee Griffin at Michigan State University describe some very encouraging work on achieving inter-rater agreement across institutions and even across that important divide between high school and college instructors (see Banta, Griffin, Flateby, and Kahn, 2009). And something very like national consensus has been demonstrated in the development of the fifteen VALUE rubrics by Terrel Rhodes and Wende Morgaine at the Association of American Colleges and Universities (http://www.aacu.org/value/).

Despite these promising developments, Charles Secolsky and Ellen Wentland remind us in the lead article in this issue that we are just beginning to consider the range of psychometric issues involved in establishing the reliability and validity that are needed to provide credibility for rubrics used in evaluating student work in electronic portfolios. Moreover, Helen Barrett (2009), now at the University of Oregon and keynote speaker for the e-portfolio track at the Assessment Institute, reminds us that there are three types of assessment of student work in e-portfolios: formative assessment of individual students' work that takes place continually and helps learners to progress, assessment for learning that uses group outcomes to glean directions for improving programs and pedagogy, and assessment of learning that is summative and intended to answer accountability questions. Barrett warns that the standardized prompts associated with assessment for accountability may turn students off, depriving us of the positive student motivation that has been so important to us in describing the advantages of e-portfolios as alternative vehicles for assessment.

The testing industry has had more than eighty years to work on such widely used standardized instruments as the SAT, yet there are still serious criticisms of even that carefully constructed test for prospective college students. How long will we need to work on the psychometric—and political—issues that must be addressed to bring e-portfolio assessment to at least a comparable level of acceptance?

In the meantime, is there any hope that we might convince governors, legislative representatives, governing boards, and federal officials that assessment to guide improvement is really the kind that adds the most value to colleges and universities? And that forcing us to accept the interpretation of accountability that focuses on measuring value added and making institutional comparisons will have us using instruments that are not capable of delivering accurate information about those things? And worst of all, that attempting to gather data that permit comparisons may cause us to focus on a narrow range of common outcomes rather than the diverse and creative outcomes that have been the distinctive hallmarks of higher education in this country?

References

Banta, T. W., Griffin, M., Flateby, T. L., & Kahn, S. (2009). *Three Promising Alternatives for Assessing College Students' Knowledge and Skills*. NILOA Occasional Paper No.2. Urbana, IL.: National Institute for Learning Outcomes Assessment, University of Illinois and Indiana University.

Barrett, H. (2009, Oct. 16). [Web log post] "Limitations of Portfolios." *E-Portfolios for Learning*. Retrieved from http://electronicportfolios.org/blog/2009/10/ limitations-of-portfolios.html

U.S. Department of Education. (2006). *A Test of Leadership: Charting the Future of U.S. Higher Education*. Washington DC: U.S. Department of Education.

Tripping Lightly Around the Globe

Assessment: A Global Phenomenon

Look for an overview of quality assurance developments in Germany, England, the Netherlands, and Mexico in 1990. From Assessment Update 2:4 (1990).

Peter Ewell and I had the extraordinary experience last summer of witnessing, in the space of just two weeks, the ways in which worldwide concerns about the quality of higher education are being played out in the West and in the East. In his column, Peter draws the outlines of the picture we saw in China. Here, I will focus on the stories told by our colleagues at the Second International Conference on Assessing Quality in Higher Education, held at St. Andrews University, Scotland.

The First International Conference had taken place in July 1989 at Cambridge University, England, with 45 individuals in attendance from nine countries. While we felt we had many common interests, we struggled to communicate—even though we all spoke English—because the terminology we use to describe our work differs (for instance, *course* in England refers to a program of study). The conference evaluation forms contained an urgent request: "Give us a glossary of terms!"

In July 1990, 80 participants representing 20 countries, armed with the glossaries we had prepared, took very little time to get acquainted and launched immediately into spirited discussions of government policies, faculty reactions, and methods of coping with calls for systematic evaluation of our work. Very recent developments in the United Kingdom and in Europe guarantee that interaction will be even more lively at the Third International Conference, scheduled for July 16–19, 1991, at Bath College of Higher Education, in England.

Ulrich Teichler, director of the Center for Research on Higher Education at the University of Kassel, told us that the quality of German universities has been assumed to be uniformly high: bright students, competent professors, and government research funds are (at least theoretically) distributed more or less equally among all German universities. In the last two years, however, the presumed cause-effect relationship between excellence in research and the production of well-prepared graduates has been questioned by the federal minister of education and in an article published in *Der Spiegel.* The latter revealed that German university students who responded to a nationwide survey gave higher ratings in some fields to new universities that lack distinguished research reputations. Teichler and his colleagues have undertaken studies designed to gather data from employers that will suggest ways to improve the academic preparation of graduates of German universities.

In most countries other than our own, as much as 90 percent of university funding is provided by the government. A theme we heard over and over at St. Andrews is that these governments are encouraging academics to establish self-study and peer-review mechanisms, which will produce qualitative judgments and recommendations that government officials can use in making policy and funding decisions.

In the United Kingdom, increasing use was made during the 1980s of peer review of the quality of research as a mechanism for determining funding levels. Now, Lewis Elton of the University of Surrey reports that the Committee of Vice-Chancellors and Principals has established two national units to help universities assess and improve the quality of teaching. The new Academic Audit Unit (AAU) will encourage each institution to define its own academic standards and build a system designed to achieve the delivery of these standards. Thus, each university will engage in its own process of self-validation, and AAU will undertake a critical review of that process. The new Universities' Staff

Development and Training Unit will provide information and advice for universities seeking ways to improve teaching and learning.

Don Westerheijden of the Center for Higher Education Policy Studies at the University of Twente, in the Netherlands, described the external evaluation system established during the last four years by the Association of Cooperating Universities in his country. Each disciplinary faculty conducts a self-evaluation. This is followed by a peer review carried out by a visiting committee, which evaluates all faculties within a given discipline in the 13-member association. Since 1988, the peer-review system has been used to effect budget reductions, with the result that recommendations have been made to terminate or consolidate a small number of programs.

Felipe Rizo of the Universidad de Aguascalientes reported that in Mexico the National Association of Universities and Institutes of Higher Education has approved a plan for internal self-studies and external peer review by visiting committees, which will be used to evaluate university programs in eight fields. In 1992, these evaluations will become an important component of the process of determining institutional funding levels.

Do these stories sound familiar? Are there any skeptics in American higher education who still believe that the call for assessment, if ignored, will go away?

Evaluation of Teaching and Learning in Germany

Look for some background on the developing interest in Germany in using student evaluations and peer review to suggest improvements at German universities. From Assessment Update 4:3 *(1992).*

Terry Smith's article about assessment in British higher education is the first of what I hope will be a growing number of *Assessment Update* pieces about international quality assessment initiatives. It's a special pleasure to know that Terry has had the opportunity to work with Peter Findlay, because all of us who attended the First International Conference on Assessing Quality in Higher Education at Cambridge University in 1989 took away very positive perceptions of the work going on at Portsmouth Polytechnic. Now *Assessment Update* readers have a chance to learn from Terry's experience there.

In February, Peter Ewell and I, along with American colleagues Tom Angelo, director of the Academic Development Center at Boston College, and Jim Wilkinson, director of the Danforth Center for Teaching and Learning at Harvard, had the extraordinary experience of addressing an assemblage of German faculty leaders on the subject of evaluating teaching and learning. The meeting was organized by HIS (Hochschul-Informations-System), sponsored by the Federal Ministry for Education and Science, and conducted in the beautifully appointed Wissenschaftszentrum (Science Center) in Bonn. Although the arrangements for this conference were not completed until December 1991, interest in evaluation in higher education is so intense in Germany that by February 20, 1992, the date of the opening session, 270 faculty, students, officials of state and federal government, and members of the press had registered.

What is behind this intense interest? First I offer a bit of background, distilled from an excellent paper by HIS associate, Edgar Frackmann, entitled "Quality Assurance in German Higher Education." By tradition, all German universities are considered to be of equal, and high, quality. Both teachers and students must meet exacting standards for entry to these institutions. Candidates for faculty positions must demonstrate their capacity for doing advanced research in their disciplines, and because they know their subject matter so well, they are presumed to be good teachers. Students must pass rigorous examinations to qualify for admission, and even with the doubling of enrollments that has occurred in German higher education since the late 1970s, only 21% of the 19- to 26-year-old age cohort participates.

Since German professors are not promoted within their own institutions, but must move to another university in order to advance, it is assumed that talent in the professoriate is rather uniformly distributed among institutions nationally. Moreover, German students traditionally have moved freely from one institution to another in completing their studies. All of this commerce among institutions promotes the assumption that individual faculty members are responsible for the quality of their own work and that individual students are responsible for their own progress through the system. German universities have not assumed responsibility for nurturing students or promoting their progress.

In the 1980s, some questions arose concerning quality in German higher education. As plans for the European Community were developing, Germans began to look beyond their borders and to assess the competitiveness of their workforce. They discovered that it was taking German students longer to complete their studies—an average of seven years for the first degree—than was the case in neighboring countries. German graduates were more than 28 years of age before they entered the labor market, and decision-makers became concerned that German youth, were spending their most creative and productive years engaged in education rather than in an occupation! Obviously, if this continued, it could impair German economic competitiveness.

The assumption of equal quality among institutions was called into question when studies revealed differences among German universities in the time it took for students pursuing the same courses of study to graduate. Moreover, as the student population increased, more attended institutions close to home, and at present fewer than 25% of university students change institutions before completing their studies. As students increasingly identify with a single university, that institution must assume more responsibility for the education and progress of its own students.

Although selected by a given university, German professors are actually employed by the state, and during the 1980s several states began to call for institutions to take more responsibility for the progress of their students and for evaluating the quality of student outcomes. In 1990, a foundation supported by German industry that had previously provided support in the form of research grants began to award prizes to universities for reducing the duration of studies for students. In a crowning blow to the assumption of equal quality, *Der Spiegel* actually published a ranking of universities based on student ratings. Encouraged by states, industry, and the press, students themselves have begun to assume leadership for developing instruments and methods to assess the quality of instruction.

The purpose of the meeting in Bonn in February was to promote interest in self-evaluation within German institutions of higher education. Examples were introduced from Great Britain and The Netherlands, where peer review models are prevalent, as well as from the United States. Despite the fact that evaluation of teaching is a relatively novel idea in Germany and is apparently being greeted with the same—dare I say even *less?*—enthusiasm by German professors as by faculty in the United States, our audience was polite. Some even exhibited genuine enthusiasm when several of us began to describe the specific evaluative methods and tools that we use. I was particularly impressed by the active involvement, including poised commentary and questioning, of the students who were present. However, I also noted an almost total absence of women (only 7 of the 270 participants were females, and several of those were graduate students, not faculty members).

As Peter Ewell and I discovered in working with faculty in China, student evaluation of instruction is the current focus of the attention being given to evaluation in Germany. Using student outcome assessment to evaluate programs, as it has been developing during the past decade in our country, is not yet fully understood or appreciated in either country. Peter, Tom, Jim, and I left Bonn exhilarated by the knowledge that we had participated in an historic first step toward that understanding in Germany. We know we will not be the last Americans invited to participate in the process of faculty development on this topic in that important country.

A Global Perspective—At Last

Look for examples of the assessment strategies various countries are adopting to address the growing worldwide concerns about higher education quality, including Total Quality Management, ISO 9000 quality audits, peer review, and performance funding. From Assessment Update 6:6 (1994).

Our Sixth International Conference on Assessing Quality in Higher Education, which was held in Hong Kong in July 1994, attracted participants from 28 countries around the world. This was our largest and most diverse audience to date, and for the first time we had significant representation from countries in the Far East in addition to Americans and Europeans. After six years of attending international conferences—all in the United Kingdom and Europe—as I listened to the featured speakers and concurrent session presenters in Hong Kong, I finally felt that I had a truly global perspective on assessment.

Worldwide there are common concerns about higher education quality stemming from similar cultural, economic, and governmental developments. Most nations are currently trying to provide higher education for the largest percentages of their populations ever to attend a college or university. Moreover, the ethnic and cultural diversity of those seeking higher education poses pedagogical challenges for the professoriate unlike any encountered previously. The costs of higher education are rising at a rate outstripped only by health care, and the resources that might once have found their way into institutions' budgets now must be spread over an increasing variety of services.

Mobility of students and faculty across national boundaries is a growing phenomenon. This prompts consideration of international standards that permit easy transfer of credits and credentials.

This is an age of consumerism. Students, parents, taxpayers, and donors want to know what they are receiving for their investment in higher education. They also want to know that education is taking place as effectively and efficiently as possible.

All of these international developments that are raising concerns about quality result in calls for assessment. And while the emphasis given to any particular approach may differ, the arrays of assessment strategies now employed in countries around the globe are becoming more similar by the day. The comprehensive philosophy of Total Quality Management (TQM), with its strong measurement component, has spread like wildfire among the colleges and universities of the world. At the Hong Kong conference, papers on TQM were presented by representatives from Australia, China, The Netherlands, South Africa, Taiwan, and the United Kingdom, as well as the United States.

In some colleges and universities where a good deal of attention is paid to the needs of industry, ISO 9000 quality audits are being conducted. This approach is used in England, New Zealand, and Singapore, for example.

Peer review has long been used by accreditation agencies and many universities in this country. More recently, peer review has become a national strategy for ensuring higher education quality in The Netherlands, Finland, and the United Kingdom. Peer review is also being considered in Japan, where universities are only beginning to come under governmental scrutiny.

Australia and Scotland are experimenting with performance funding. Chile has joined the countries of Europe in the search for national indicators of performance.

Although many of the conference presentations in Hong Kong had as their focus national quality-assurance initiatives designed to serve accountability purposes, I find far more interesting the campus-specific assessment approaches designed for improvement purposes that are being carried out in the United Kingdom and in this country. While it seems to me that the national resources available for faculty development in the United Kingdom must be the best in the world, the U.S. capacity for institutional research, including assessment, is enviable. These strengths, combined with many other cultural and economic factors in the United Kingdom and the United States, have produced the world's most advanced, specialized, and improvement-oriented assessment practice.

I am currently immersed in reviewing nearly 200 institutional case studies in assessment for a new book, the contents of which will be discussed in future issues of *Assessment Update*. My observation above about specialized, improvement-oriented assessment practice in the United States is based not only on reading and hearing the Hong Kong conference papers but also on the work with cases for the book. What I am seeing is an increasing number of creative evaluation studies undertaken by faculty who employ their research skills to conduct assessment in their own disciplines. The result is specific, detailed information about gaps in student learning, deficits in fundamental skills, and problems with the student services provided on campuses. This is the best information yet gathered for directing improvements.

Some of the articles in this issue of *Assessment Update* illustrate my points. In the lead article, Patricia D. Murphy describes one institution's answer to the often-asked question, "How do we assess student outcomes in graduate programs?" Very simply, faculty in various disciplines are beginning to state desired learning outcomes more explicitly, then rate the extent to which they see those outcomes attained in course assignments, comprehensive written and oral exams, and theses—all the traditional methods of assessing the individual accomplishments of graduate students. The difference now is that in addition to a pass/fail notation or letter grade on an individual transcript, graduate faculty have specific data that can be aggregated across students and compared with their stated goals to ascertain where students are most successful and where some new method or methods might be needed to remedy a deficiency in learning.

The tool used by graduate faculty at North Dakota State University to add new purpose to the assessment of student learning is described by Murphy as "a simple rating scale" attached to each desired learning outcome. In their article, Peter A. Facione and Noreen C. Facione tell us about one such simple rating scale that they have devised to assess critical thinking ability as manifested in students' essays, course assignments, projects, and performances. If faculty can use this scale to assess something as complex and difficult to define as critical thinking, and graduate faculty can apply similar scales in assessing the advanced attainments of Ph.D. students, we may be witnessing a giant leap forward in assessment technology—developed not by measurement specialists but by faculty who are employing their research skills to solve assessment problems in their own disciplines.

Serendipity has brought together in this issue one study that resulted in the definition of a problem and another that suggests a potential solution to that problem. We already had a full issue that included Anita Gandolfo's article on why students do not go to class when the attendance policy article by William E. McMullin and Jon M. Young arrived in the mail. We made room for the two to appear together. Both articles are based on carefully designed evaluation research conducted by faculty who employed their disciplinary investigative expertise.

William S. Moore, guest Community College Strategies columnist, describes the Student Voices Project, a collaborative research project involving six institutions in the state of Washington in a study designed to enhance "understanding of how students evaluate their learning experiences." This is yet another example of faculty applying their research skills to create innovative approaches to assessment. And Moore promises more of this. He says that the Student Voices Project should "provide colleges with a model for further qualitative studies on other student populations."

In my last column, I promised something in each issue for newcomers to assessment. Peter J. Gray's Campus Profiles column describes Chicago State University's first initiative in assessment. In addition, William J. Struhar's article is an entertaining description of the process of preparing to assess student outcomes in general education. (He does think it's possible to tame that beast!)

———————————

The Most Compelling
International Dialogue to Date

Look for brief descriptions of the quality assurance topics discussed by delegates from 26 countries attending a conference in Manchester, England, in 1999. From Assessment Update *11:6 (1999).*

The Eleventh International Conference on Assessing Quality in Higher Education, cosponsored by Indiana University-Purdue University Indianapolis and H & E Associates and hosted by the University of Salford, was held July 23 to 25, 1999, in Manchester, England. The audience was the most diverse ever, composed of delegates from twenty-six countries. For the first time in the history of this conference, there were representatives of Nepal, India, Nigeria, Kenya, and Botswana, as well as several historically black universities in South Africa. Conversations in the special interest groups (on assessment as related to teaching and learning, on faculty development, on institutional effectiveness, on workforce and vocational education, on TQM, and on quality assurance policy) were more lively and intense than ever before.

In the opening plenary session, John Sanger, pro vice-chancellor of the University of Salford, provided an overview of issues surrounding quality and standards in higher education in England. He reminded us that since 1989 the proportion of eighteen-year-olds entering higher education in England has more than doubled—from 15 percent to more than 30 percent. But during the same period, funding from the government per student enrolled has been reduced in real terms by 35 percent. With growing numbers of mature students and members of minority groups, in addition to more eighteen-year-olds, seeking higher education, the range of qualifications of entering students is broader than it has ever been. According to Sanger, a recent study shows that faculty salaries are generally lower than market medians, in some areas by as much as 30 percent. A young lecturer at a university in London earns no more than a London bus driver. But at the same time, academic staff face substantially increased teaching loads, fewer support staff, and insufficient funding to replace aging equipment and maintain buildings.

Neither the Major nor Blair governments has been willing to increase funding for higher education. In fact, in the current year and for the next two, the level of funding is being cut 1 percent each year. Despite these cuts, the Blair government has announced goals to increase and widen participation, to educate students for the workforce, and to encourage lifelong learning while enhancing quality. Institutional strategies for counteracting the effects of these developments include recruiting more overseas students and increasing the income from grants and contracts and from partnerships with business and industry.

In 1997, the Quality Assurance Agency (QAA) was established in Britain to bring together the responsibilities for institution-based quality audit and subject-based teaching quality assessment. These two sets of activities had developed in isolation, thus requiring much duplication of time, effort, and paperwork on the part of institutions attempting to comply with the requirements of both. Details of the process the QAA will use to combine these assessment activities are still being worked out, in part because, according to Sanger, "The exercise has proved to be a difficult one . . . especially in terms of being able to navigate the fine line between defining the appropriate standard with a sufficient degree of detail to be of practical value on the one hand, and specifying what is in effect a 'national curriculum' on the other." In this issue of *Assessment Update*, George Gordon describes how one institution in the British system, the University of Strathclyde in Scotland, has attempted to combine institution-based and subject-based assessment in an overall quality assurance strategy.

In the Commonwealth keynote address, John Fielden, director of the Commonwealth Higher Education Management Service, explained the benchmarking activities of a consortium of institutions working together in the newly formed Commonwealth Universities' Management Benchmarking Club. In the same session, Vin Massaro, director of his own management consulting firm in Australia, shared his views on quality assurance in transnational education.

The European keynote focused on the first year of the EQUIS Project, which is designed to provide an approval process for management schools. The speaker was Gordon Shenton, director of EQUIS, a program of the European Foundation for Management Development in Brussels. Dean Hubbard, president of Northwest Missouri State University, was the U.S. keynote speaker. He reviewed the influence of the total quality movement on U.S. institutions in the 1990s, including recent initiatives by several regional accrediting agencies to incorporate elements of the Malcolm Baldrige National Quality Award standards in their accreditation guidelines.

In my column "What's New in Assessment?" (Banta, 1999) I reported that the sessions at the 1999 AAHE Assessment Conference were dominated by presentations on assessment in general education, major fields, and institutional effectiveness. The American papers presented at the conference in England focused on the same themes. However, an equal number of papers originating in other countries also addressed these themes, emphasizing their global importance.

But the largest proportion of papers presented in Manchester by academics from countries other than the United States addressed issues of national quality assurance policy. This is not at all surprising because most other countries have national higher education systems. Thus national policy trumps individual state policies. In the United States, states have been the major players in quality assurance.

Some of the papers that caught my attention in Manchester addressed these topics: evaluating the quality of teaching and research in Scotland, applying TQM and ISO 9000 standards in higher education in England and Scotland, the trend toward emphasizing vocational education in universities in India, assessing students' teamwork skills in Australia and group work in Germany, ensuring the quality of distance education in the United Kingdom, and overcoming the difficulties in assessing quality in higher education institutions in South Africa. I hope you can forgive my partiality, but I thought two of the best papers were written by Ann L. McCann and Douglas M. Scheidt of the United States. McCann provided evidence that the activities of the

Assessment Center for Health Professions Education, which she directs at the Baylor College of Dentistry, have increased the capabilities of the director of five model sites to define competence for their students, develop appropriate assessment instruments, and use the results of assessment to improve curricula and instruction. Scheidt, an assistant professor in the Department of Health Sciences at SUNY Brockport, described the use of competence-based student self-assessment and curricular review in program evaluation in professional education. A licensed psychologist, Scheidt has been particularly careful in examining the psychometric properties of the several instruments used in his department's assessment program.

The final plenary session at the conference in England featured a panel discussion of issues identified in the special interest groups, which met on three occasions during the three-day conference. One of the major issues was raised by delegates from developing countries. They asked how indigenous universities in their countries, such as historically black universities in South Africa, can survive if European and American universities bring their courses to those countries and thus establish standards of quality that the indigenous institutions cannot meet.

We were not able to respond adequately to this question in Manchester. We resolved to address it in the program of the Twelfth International Conference on Assessing Quality in Higher Education, to be hosted by the Royal Melbourne Institute of Technology, June 28 to 30, 2000, at the Ibis Hotel in Melbourne, Australia.

References

Banta, T. W. (1999). Editor's Notes: What's New in Assessment? *Assessment Update*, *11*(5), 3, 11.

Sanger, J. (1999). Keynote address at the Eleventh International Conference on Assessing Quality in Higher Education. July 23–25, 1999. Manchester, England.

Two Conferences, Two Systems— Similar Perspectives?

Look for the contrast between themes—"The End of Quality" and "A Shared Commitment"—being discussed at quality assessment conferences in England in 2001 and the U.S. in 2002, respectively. From Assessment Update 14:6 (2002).

As I began to prepare some remarks for our 14th International Conference on Assessing Quality in Higher Education—held this year in Vienna, Austria—I surrounded myself with journals published in the United Kingdom and Europe. I hoped to gain a current perspective on the responses of academics in other Western countries to the pervasive need to provide evidence of their accountability to external stakeholders.

My attention was drawn immediately to the April 2002 issue of *Quality in Higher Education*, in which the editor, Lee Harvey, director of the Center for Research and Quality at the University of Central England, had summarized the major themes and conclusions of a conference with the provocative title, "The End of Quality." Harvey had organized this conference at his institution in Birmingham, England, in May 2001.

According to Harvey (2002), three principal themes emerged during the conference in Birmingham:

1. Has external quality review had its day?

2. Has control of quality been usurped by market forces and information technology?

3. Does the development of mass higher education necessarily mean the end of quality?

Understanding each of these themes requires a bit more elaboration. In the United Kingdom and Europe, where higher education has been highly regulated by national governments, external quality review means an audit or evaluation conducted by a government ministry, professional body, or special agency. Since governments in most countries historically have limited access to higher education to the best-prepared 10–15 percent of young people, academics in the United Kingdom and Europe understandably are concerned about the impact on quality of government policies of the past decade that have pushed the college-going rate to 50 percent or higher. With increasing recognition worldwide that higher education is an important determinant of economic development, higher education has become a big business with many alternative providers, some using technology to extend their reach across national boundaries. Will the world market ultimately become the arbiter of quality in higher education?

Delegates to the End of Quality conference had some opinions about quality monitoring that surfaced right away! They said that it adds to the bureaucracy that already burdens higher education and that the need for detailed documentation creates extra work for which no one has time. It asks the wrong questions, focuses on accountability rather than improvement, and produces only short-term responses that have no lasting impact, particularly on student learning in individual classrooms.

The critics advanced additional arguments against external quality assessment as they have come to know it: Resources that might be used to improve teaching and learning are diverted to fulfill evaluation requirements. The threat that government funds will be cut causes some to manipulate data to conceal weaknesses or to engage in academic gamesmanship. Finally, paranoia about the pernicious effects of external monitoring is beginning to shift to cynicism that after all the time-consuming effort and expense, nothing important will happen.

Having attended the June 2002 assessment conference sponsored by the American Association for Higher Education (AAHE) in Boston just the month before traveling to Vienna, I could not help drawing some comparisons between what I observed there and Lee Harvey's summary of what had transpired at the End of Quality conference. While external pressures on colleges and universities to demonstrate accountability began at roughly the same time in the United States as in the United Kingdom and Europe, U.S. institutions enjoy far more autonomy and have not been subjected to the same level of external quality monitoring that academics in the United Kingdom have experienced recently.

The contrast between the tenor of presentations at the End of Quality conference and the assessment conference in Boston, which was titled "Assessment: A Shared Commitment," was stark. The principal theme among participants in Boston was "How can we use assessment to improve teaching and learning?" Sessions addressed methods for assessing student achievement in general education—in writing, critical thinking, speaking, and information literacy—as well as in the major. The assessment method that seemed to be drawing most attention was the electronic portfolio, in which students take responsibility for selecting samples of their own work, then writing accompanying reflective essays to explain how their choices illustrate that they have attained specified knowledge and skills.

For participants in Boston, interest in methods for assessing institutional effectiveness was second only to that in improving student learning. Sessions addressed such questions as the following: What evidence can demonstrate that we are fulfilling our institutional mission? How should we prepare for a visit from our regional accrediting association? How might we compete for the Baldrige Award? How can we develop a culture of assessment—engaging faculty, using results, involving our stakeholders?

Gauging the impact of student participation in cocurricular activities was another theme at the AAHE conference. How can we assess our efforts to develop the whole student? What methods can tell us what we are achieving with learning communities and first-year seminars? How can we assess the effects of advising?

The AAHE conference developers created a segment on "assessing the ineffable." Sessions in this track provided ideas for assessing student development in such difficult-to-measure areas as academic integrity, creativity, diversity, ethics, gender differences, spirituality, and values.

As I have observed the development of outcomes assessment in the United States, it seems to me that faculty and administrators have developed far more positive and constructive attitudes over the years. At assessment conferences in the late 1980s and early 1990s, the questions we asked included the following: Why do we have to prove ourselves through assessment? What do states and accreditors want of us? How can we meet external demands with minimal effort and disruption? In 2002 our questions seem to be, What are the most promising methods for assessing learning? student development (in its broadest sense)? institutional effectiveness? How can we broaden campus participation in assessment and fully realize its promise for continually improving higher education?

Are we seeing the end of quality? No; even colleagues attending the conference in England reached that conclusion. Is interest in improving the quality of higher education on the wane? Absolutely not. In fact, one might argue that interest worldwide has never been greater and is increasing daily.

Would our activities and approaches to assessment in the United States be more like those of academics on the other side of the Atlantic if our federal government were much more involved in institutional quality monitoring than is the case today? We may have an opportunity to find out. The press to assess was exerted on the K–12 education sector in this country nearly two decades before it reached higher education. As we observe the impact of the No Child Left Behind Act of 2001 (NCLB) and contemplate suggestions that the National Assessment of Educational Progress (NAEP) be administered annually in grades 3 through 8 in every state in order to "level the playing field" when gauging state-by-state progress toward NCLB goals (Linn, Baker, and Betebenner, 2002), it is impossible not to wonder if proposals for national testing to monitor levels of college student learning can be far behind.

References

Harvey, L. (2002). The End of Quality? *Quality in Higher Education, 8*(1), 5–22.

Linn, R. L., Baker, E. L., & Betebenner, D. W. (2002). Accountability Systems: Implications of Requirements of the No Child Left Behind Act of 2001. *Educational Researcher, 31*(6), 3–16.

Sour Notes from Europe

Look for some criticisms of the Bologna Process by European faculty and students presenting their perspectives at an international conference in Vilnius, Lithuania in 2009. From Assessment Update *21:6 (2009).*

I am writing this column as I return from Vilnius, Lithuania, site of the 31st annual meeting of the European Association for Institutional Research (EAIR). I have attended almost all of the EAIR conferences since 1990, and because the attendance is usually just 300 or so, it is possible to have extended conversations during the meeting with individuals who share one's interests. Thus, I look forward to this annual opportunity to see many people with whom I have exchanged ideas about assessment in previous years.

Just before and during my flights to Vilnius, several assessment coordinators who contribute to the ASSESS listserv in the United States were describing their experiences with ad hominem attacks by faculty colleagues. That is, some faculty members are reacting so negatively to the call to conduct assessment of student learning outcomes that they are launching personal, public verbal attacks on assessment coordinators who are trying to explain their campus's approach to assessment. I find the fact that some would so like to kill the messenger a full thirty years into the history of outcomes assessment in our country profoundly discouraging. Because I must admit that this e-mail discussion about the deterioration of civility in our country may have colored my view of the sessions I attended in Vilnius, I offer the following as a series of impressions. I will not even identify most of the presenters, in case others were hearing a more positive message from them than I did.

The first conference session I selected was presented by two academics from the United Kingdom who argued that quality assurance, which we would call *outcomes assessment*, is naturally resented by academic staff (faculty) because it is being imposed by external authorities—that is, governments or accrediting agencies. Their proposed solution is to provide administrative support to encourage faculty in individual departments to determine how they will approach outcomes assessment. I felt as if I had stepped back to 1980; isn't this kind of departmental autonomy in structuring assessment just what we have been advocating ever since then?

Next, I chose a session presented by a leading European quality assessment scholar whose papers are always provocative. His presentation at EAIR did not disappoint in that regard. He described the evolution of quality culture at universities over the past two decades, then argued that too little tangible benefit has resulted, given all the time and treasure that has been invested in trying to create that culture. He suggested that more benefit could have been realized if that investment had been directed to faculty development instead. That triggered a flashback for me: In 1992, I was invited by leaders in the U.S. Department of Education to write a paper advising them on their plans to develop a national test of generic skills for college students. I, of course, argued against developing such a test, but I went on to say that if this investment were to be made—and I had been assured that the intention of the leaders at that time was to do just that—it should be accompanied by a faculty development initiative so massive that its scope and cost would rival that invested in the Manhattan Project that produced the first atomic bomb.

In Vilnius, I selected four presentations that focused on the Bologna Process, in particular on *tuning*, the initiative that is attempting to bring academics in various disciplines together to develop common student learning outcomes in each discipline across universities in various European countries. The intention of tuning is to make standards for a degree in a given subject sufficiently comparable that students can move across country boundaries to pursue their studies in a particular subject and employers can expect students with degrees from various universities in a range of European countries to bring similar knowledge and skills to the workplace.

Instead of harmony, I heard a series of sour notes about tuning. Lesley Wilson, secretary general of the European University Association, said in her plenary address that there has been "relatively poor involvement of academics" in the Bologna Process. So far, the process has created as much diversity—branding, profile building, competition—among universities both within and across countries as it has produced subject-specific convergence.

Then I listened as speakers from two different countries outlined the "pitfalls and dangers" of specifying learning outcomes for degree programs. Their principal argument was that stating outcomes would narrow the curriculum. One speaker expressed the fear that only outcomes that would lend themselves to being assessed would be chosen. (Does this sound familiar?) The other voiced the fear that the outcomes would focus on learning taking place in formal education only as opposed to the informal learning settings outside the classroom, in which much valuable human learning takes place.

Lest I convey the impression that I left Vilnius totally dejected about the prospects for ever succeeding in engaging most faculty colleagues in assessing student learning outcomes as an integral part of improving teaching and learning, let me tell you about one more session. In an effort to encourage younger colleagues to present their research at EAIR meetings, the association has initiated an award for the best paper presented by someone under the age of thirty-five. The winners in 2009 were four *undergraduates* from the University of Freiburg in Germany! They also are disillusioned by their experience with the effects of the Bologna Process as they pursue bachelor's degrees in psychology at Freiburg. They said that their curriculum is so prescribed that they have no freedom to choose courses and no opportunity to study abroad if they want to complete their degree on time. They study forty hours a week and still are not acquiring what they consider "practical competences."

These four students decided to use what they called "Obama-style community organizing" to attract faculty attention to their concerns. They found a community organizing tool kit and, following the directions, established a vision for their work, created awareness and solicited ideas by using bulletin boards on campus, held community meetings, and established working groups. Their vision is to correct problems created by the Bologna Process. One of the four working groups focuses on curriculum and another on competences to be developed in the psychology degree program. In response to questions, the students admitted that it was not difficult to attract faculty support for their cause "because Bologna is also viewed negatively by faculty." But here is my cause for hope: the students said that faculty are beginning to pay attention to the work coming out of their group focused on competences. Students wrote their own learning outcomes, and faculty are considering their list. Perhaps it is *our students* who will in the future be most effective in engaging faculty in assessing student learning outcomes as a component of enhancing teaching and learning!